GLASGOW

THE OFFICIAL GUIDE

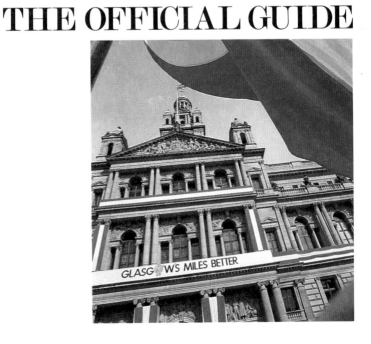

GLASG🌹WS MILES BETTER

ISEABAIL MACLEOD

GW00371034

RICHARD DREW PUBLISHING
GLASGOW

First published 1987 by
Richard Drew Publishing Limited
6 Clairmont Gardens, Glasgow G3 7LW
Scotland

British Library Cataloguing in Publication Data

MacLeod, Iseabail
  Glasgow: the official guide.
  1. Glasgow (Strathclyde)——Description——Guide-books
  I. Title
  914.14′4304858   DA890.G5

ISBN 0-86267-190-6

Designed by Westpoint

Maps by Reg and Marjorie Piggott

Photographs by Douglas Corrance and the
Scottish Tourist Board with additional photography by
Alan Crumlish (p 74); Larry Cuffe (pp 4/5, 27 lower, 51,
63 top, 85); Edinburgh Picture Library (pp 9, 25 left);
Glasgow Art Gallery and Museum (pp 34, 35);
Hunterian Art Gallery (p 39 left); Graham Lees (p 53);
Scottish Development Agency (p 31 lower).

Set in Medieval by John Swain Ltd Glasgow
Printed and bound in Scotland by
Blantyre Printing and Binding Co. Ltd.

GLASGOW

THE OFFICIAL GUIDE

The Publisher would like to thank Glasgow District Council and the Greater Glasgow Tourist Board for their help and advice in the publication of this guide.

CONTENTS

Efforts have been made to mark with the now accepted sign ♿ premises which have facilities for the disabled.

Numbers in margin indicate position of places of interest on map on pages 16/17.

INTRODUCTION

Glasgow is Scotland's largest city with a current population of about 740,000. It is also the main town of Strathclyde Region where 2.6 million people, half the population of Scotland, live. It has a dramatic setting, spanning a wide river and built on a series of hills which afford panoramic vistas of the city itself and of its surroundings; these include some of the most beautiful scenery to be found anywhere.

The city has changed many times in the eight centuries of its existence, from a little town with only ecclesiastical significance in the Middle Ages to a prosperous and beautiful city in the 17th and 18th centuries, to a rich but over-crowded industrial sprawl in the 19th, to a stone-cleaned, forward-looking city in the late 20th.

For a time it was the second city of the British Empire and there is no continent which has not benefited from the ingenuity, enterprise, skill, inventiveness, and even genius of people born or trained in Glasgow. Its ships sailed every sea, its locomotives pulled the trains on every continent, the industry of the world ran on its engines, and its carpets rolled across the floors of the world's exotic places.

Looking north over Glasgow from Queen's Park

For more than five centuries Glasgow University has turned out graduates who have gone all over the world to distinguish themselves in every field of human endeavour. The university has the oldest engineering school in the world and the largest medical school in Britain.

Plaque showing site at the Old College (University of Glasgow)

In much of this century, despite the warmth of its people, outsiders have tended to have a jaundiced view of Glasgow, not always without justification; like any other major city it has not been without its problems. In the past few years however new attitudes have prevailed and the city's life, as well as its image, have been improved to such an extent that in 1986 the Ministers of Culture of the 12 member states of the European Economic Community de-cided that Glasgow would be European city of culture in 1990; that Glasgow's claim was superior to Bath, Bristol, Cardiff, Cambridge, Edinburgh, Leeds, Liverpool, and Swansea, who had all made submissions for the title; that Glasgow was good enough to rank with Athens, Florence, Amsterdam, Berlin, and Paris, holders of the title up to 1990; that Glasgow was a city of song, dance, drama, poetry, classical, jazz and pop music, of architectural beauty, imagination, enterprise, and daring.

In 1988 the world will beat a path to its door for the Glasgow Garden Festival (see p. 10) which will run from April to September; it is expected to generate many millions of pounds of investment and to attract between three and four million visitors. Its site is on the south bank of the river Clyde opposite the Scottish Exhibition and Conference Centre.

SECC

The £36 million exhibition centre (see p. 86) was opened in 1985 and in December 1986, it was declared 'the best exhibition centre in the world' by readers of *Conferences and Exhibitions International,* one of the leading publications in the industry. The Glasgow centre was chosen ahead of venues in London, Las Vegas, and Helsinki. Previous winners of the award were the Pompidou Arts Centre in Paris and the National Exhibition Centre in Birmingham. An £18 million hotel to be built by Forum Hotels International near the SEEC will be opened in 1988.

The SEEC replaces the Kelvin Hall, once the largest exhibition hall in Scotland. Work on a £6 million conversion of Kelvin Hall into a major indoor sports stadium (see p. 80) and transport museum (see p. 39) is scheduled to be completed in 1988 to coincide with the opening of the Garden Festival.

A large number of people have been working for a long time to enhance the quality of life in Glasgow; politicians, administrators, organisers, heads of industry and commerce, traders, designers, artists, musicians, dreamers, people with ideas, and people with money.

Among the things which have helped to make the new Glasgow has been the dramatic change in the appearance of the city by the cleaning of public and private buildings (made possible by the results of the Clean Air Act), by the building of massive new hotels, office blocks, shopping centres, the clearing of derelict sheds on the banks of the Clyde to create two miles of attractive walkway. Glasgow was one of the first cities to realise the value of rehabilitating some of its older buildings and many crumbling tenements have thus been made into fine modern dwellings. Other factors of

Stone-cleaned terrace in West End

improvement have included the control of air pollution, the mounting of art exhibitions of international importance, the organisation of one of the largest marathons in the world, the city council's massive support of the visual and performing arts, and the improvement of road and rail communications with the rest of Britain.

As a business centre Glasgow ranks high and at the time of writing investment in commercial projects in the city is running at more than £1 billion. Glasgow has the only American Chamber of Commerce in the UK outside London. The city also houses the headquarters of the Scottish Development

Towers of Hutchesons' Hospital Hall and City Chambers

Stock Exchange House reflected in Clydesdale Bank

Agency, Clydesdale Bank, Scottish Trades Union Congress, Scottish Stock Exchange, Scottish Amicable Life Assurance Society, Scottish Mutual Assurance Society, Scottish office of the Confederation of British Industry, as well as branch offices of every major insurance company in Britain, and branches of banks of Nova Scotia, China, Pakistan, and Ireland.

Above all Glasgow is known for its warmth and friendliness, not only to the visitor but to the stranger in its midst. It has absorbed many new elements in its population, thousands of Highlanders and Irish in search of work in the 19th century, Jewish immigrants and numerous Italians, and more recently Indians and Pakistanis and many others. All have settled and, while retaining some of their own culture, have added to the pattern of living in this most Scottish of cities.

Glasgow
Garden Festival '88

The **Glasgow Garden Festival '88** will be the most important event in Glasgow for several decades. Investment will run to over £36 million and backers include the Scottish Development Agency (the Festival's main planner and management agency), Glasgow District Council, Strathclyde Regional Council, The Scottish Tourist Board, and commercial organisations.

The site, of well over 100 acres at Princes Dock on the south side of the river, is directly opposite the new Scottish Exhibition and Conference Centre (see p. 86). A new bridge is being built to join the two sites, which will have excellent transport links by road, rail and air. During the six months of the Festival (April to September), the SECC will run a series of related events, including conferences, exhibitions, and sporting events.

Glasgow District Council has committed a further £500 000 to organise entertainments, sporting and cultural events to create a citywide festival atmosphere during 1988.

The Festival's aims go beyond the purely horticultural and, in addition to spectacular displays of plants, it will embrace six theme zones;

water and maritime with the Clyde as a main focus for boat trips and water sports, and displays of water at work.

recreation and sport linked to the above, various outdoor sport for all ages will be featured.

landscape and scenery a range of Scottish scenery will be exhibited, with a special emphasis on plants and wildlife.

plants and food many aspects of gardening will be covered, as well as food production on a larger scale in agriculture.

health and well-being theme gardens will show the link between plants and health and there will be displays of physical fitness, conservation etc.

science and technology as well as aspects of the science of plant growing, there will be displays of modern technology in, for example, sources of energy.

There will also be three theme trails, covering **History and Heritage, Horticulture**, and **Education and Culture**, as well as ample facilities for shopping, entertainment and catering, many of them integrated with the above themes.

BRIEF HISTORY OF THE CITY

According to legend, Glasgow has its origins in the sixth century, in the community founded by its patron, Saint Mungo or Kentigern, on the banks of the Molendinar Burn, a small tributary of the Clyde which now runs mainly underground. 'Glasgow', as befitted its original position, most probably means 'green hollow' in the Celtic language (akin to modern Welsh) of the Britons, who inhabited the area at that time. The popular explanation of the name as 'dear green place' may originate from the *Life of Saint Kentigern* by the twelfth-century Bishop Jocelin, whose Latin text explains it as 'dear community'.

There are many legends attached to the story of St Mungo. His mother Thenew (later corrupted to Enoch) was banished by her father, the king of Lothian, when she was found to be pregnant by a Cumbrian prince. The little boat in which she was cast adrift in the Firth of Forth came to land at Culross in Fife and there her son was born. The child was taken in and educated as a priest by St Serf and the monks of his Celtic monastery. Eventually Mungo set out on a mission and on the way stopped at the house of a holy man, Fergus, who was near death. Mungo, charged with burying Fergus, put the body on a cart drawn by two wild bulls, to be carried to a place ordained by the Lord. The cart stopped on a little hill above the Molendinar Burn where he buried Fergus and built a church and monastic settlement.

The elements in Glasgow's coat of arms are all connected with legends of St Mungo; they are remembered in an old rhyme:

> There's the tree that never grew,
> There's the bird that never flew;
> There's the fish that never swam,
> There's the bell that never rang.

Bowl showing Glasgow Coat of Arms (People's Palace)

The legends however fail to fit the rhyme. Mungo as a boy is said to have kindled a fire with a frozen tree branch; he also revived a pet bird which his companions had killed. Another story tells of a queen who gave a ring, a present from her husband, to her lover, a knight of the court. The king found the ring on the man's hand as he slept during a hunt. He threw the ring into the river and then demanded it back from the queen on pain of execution. In despair she asked Mungo for help and he sent a monk to fish in the river; the man caught a salmon with the ring in its mouth. In the Middle Ages the city possessed 'St Mungo's Bell', which may have been given to him on his ordination as a bishop.

Bishop Jocelin played an important role in the history of the city; in 1175 he secured a burgh charter from King William the Lion, allowing his burgh to hold a market every Thursday. A second charter gave it the right to hold a fair every July, a practice which in one form or other has continued to the present time. Today the middle weekend of July is observed as a public holiday, still known as the 'Glasgow Fair' and the following two weeks, known as 'Fair Fortnight', are still the normal annual holiday of many factories and works.

In spite of its status as a burgh of regality, Glasgow in the Middle Ages was little more than a village which was an important ecclesiastical and academic centre. Glasgow Cathedral (see p. 18), most of whose present fabric dates back to the 13th century, is now the only Gothic building in Scotland which has remained roofed and has been used for public worship throughout the centuries of its existence; the University of Glasgow (see p. 52), founded in 1451, is the second oldest in Scotland and fourth oldest in Britain.

The city began to rise out of its medieval slumber in the 17th century but even in 1723, it was described by Daniel Defoe as 'The beautifullest little city I have seen in Britain'. Its real climb to prosperity began around this time, partly owing to increased trade with the Colonies which followed the Treaty of Union with England in 1707. By the 1720s Glasgow was taking over some of the trade of English ports such as Bristol, Liverpool and Whitehaven. One of the chief imports was sugar and Glasgow became the centre of the sugar industry in Scotland. The most spectacular development in trade was however that in tobacco with Virginia and the merchants who thus rose in the world became known as the Tobacco Lords.

One of Glasgow's problems as a trading city was the shallowness of the Clyde. This was at least partially solved in the late 18th century by a scheme in which the river below Glasgow was narrowed by means of jetties, thus increasing the current and facilitating dredging to deepen the riverbed. These measures allowed Glasgow to become a deep-water port, and helped it to survive when its trade was being threatened by the American War of Independence.

With the Industrial Revolution commercial advance was followed by a rise in industrial enterprise which made Glasgow the prosperous but overcrowded city it became in the 19th century. The main industries were textiles and chemicals, and later shipbuilding,

Shipbuilding on the Clyde

but Glasgow developed a wide range of heavy industry, based ultimately on local coal and iron ore. Cheap raw materials lay at the heart of the industrial advantage which made Glasgow the 'Second City' and workshop of the British Empire. Another factor was cheap labour from the thousands of immigrants who swelled the population, especially from the Highlands and Islands and from Ireland. The city's population grew apace, rising from 28 000 in 1765, to 202 000 in 1831 and 1 088 000 in 1931. Post-war decline in industry and also the movement of large numbers of inhabitants to new towns and developing suburbs has caused a dramatic drop in recent years and the population in 1984 was about 740 000, more or less an ideal size for a large city.

The medieval city clustered closely round the Cathedral on the banks of the Molendinar Burn. In the 17th and 18th centuries, with expanding trade and wealth, it began to grow north-west and south-west. The 18th-century merchant city expanded west, but throughout the century, the city remained largely north of the river. The first major expansion of the 19th century however took place on the south side, when Gorbals and Lauriston were first developed between 1800 and 1830. This area had a short life as an expensive suburb, since quite soon improving transport allowed development even further out and the Gorbals fell into decay.

Prosperous Victorians moved first of all to what is now Charing Cross and beyond, and from there

**Plate showing
Cathedral (People's
Palace)**

to Hillhead and the environs of the Botanic Gardens (laid out in 1842), to which district the University moved in 1870 (see p. 52). From the early 20th century expensive housing has tended to be built around

Victorian tenement in Broomhill

Tiled close

the periphery. The coming of passenger railways from the 1830s opened up new possibilities for excursions, holidays and eventually early commuting so that many prosperous Glaswegians had homes on the Clyde coast, either permanent or for holidays.

Overcrowded city living in 19th-century Britain caused enormous health problems with the spread of disease, including epidemics of cholera and typhus, but these were greatly alleviated in Glasgow by an enlightened water policy. In the 1850s a new scheme brought water from Loch Katrine in the Trossachs (see p. 62) to the city, giving it probably the best water supply in the country. As well as improving the health of the inhabitants, it encouraged enterprises such as distilling, which became a major industry in the late 19th century.

Around the turn of the 20th century, Glasgow's administrative boundaries stretched to engulf independent burghs such as Govanhill, Govan, Partick and Hillhead. With local-government reorganisation of Scotland in 1975, the City became the City of Glasgow District within Strathclyde Region. Both the District and the Regional headquarters are in Glasgow, the former in the City Chambers (see p. 26) and the latter in India Street.

City Chambers

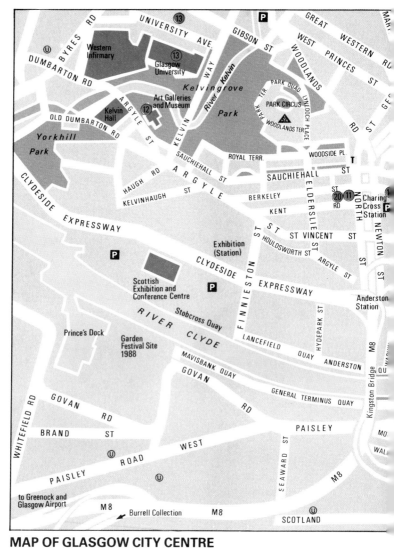

MAP OF GLASGOW CITY CENTRE

**KEY TO
PLACES OF INTEREST**

1. Provand's Lordship
2. Glasgow Cathedral
3. Tolbooth Steeple
4. Tron Steeple/
   Tron Theatre

5. Hutchesons' Hospital Hall
6. Trades House
7. City Chambers
8. Greater Glasgow Tourist Information Centre
9. Stirling's Library
10. Willow Tearoom

11. Mitchell Library
12. Art Gallery and Museum, Kelvingrove
13. Hunterian Museum and Art Gallery
14. People's Palace
15. Tenement House
16. Third Eye Centre
17. City Halls/ Ticket Centre

18. Citizens' Theatre
19. King's Theatre
20. Mitchell Theatre
21. Pavilion Theatre
22. Theatre Royal
23. Glasgow School of Art

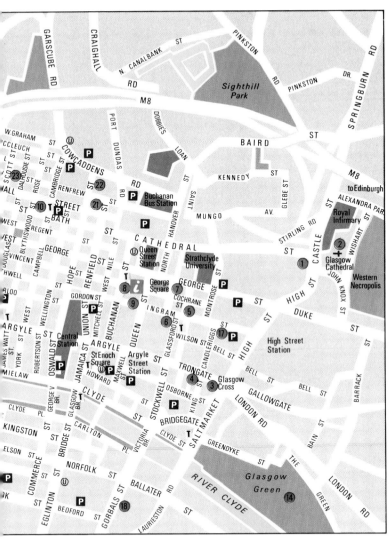

Ⓤ   Underground station

🅿   Car Park

Ⱦ   Public lavatory

/////   Pedestrian precinct

𝒊   Greater Glasgow Tourist Information Centre

SYHA   Youth Hostel

TOUR OF THE CITY CENTRE (EAST)

The route eastward from public transport terminals at Queen Street railway station and Buchanan Bus Station takes us past the University of Strathclyde and several other important educational establishments (see p. 53). Cathedral Street passes through Townhead, one of the early areas of expansion in the growing Glasgow of the 18th century. Above a sliproad to the M8 Motorway is **Martyrs' Public School**, a good example of Charles Rennie Mackintosh's architectural style. Closed as a school in 1976, it is now on lease to the Forum Arts Society Trust and is to be developed as an arts and recreation centre.

Near the end of Cathedral Street, on the corner of Macleod Street and Castle Street is **Provand's Lordship**, the only pre-Reformation dwelling house left in the city. It was built in 1471 as part of the Hospital of St Nicholas (a refuge for the poor), probably as a house for the Master or Preceptor and other Cathedral clergy. Part of it soon after became the home of one of their number, the Prebendary of Barlanark, whose income came from the lands (or lordship) or Provand of Provan, a little to the east of the city; see Provan Hall (p. 57). After the Reformation it came into private hands and in 1670 it was extended by the then owner, Wil-

Plaque, Provand's Lordship

liam Bryson. In the early 20th century it was rescued from demolition by a group of interested people. Today it is a Glasgow museum, housing mainly medieval material (as well as an early 20th century sweetie shop on the ground floor).

Opposite is **Glasgow Cathedral**, once the dominant central building of a small community, now slightly swamped by its rather massive surroundings, including the early 20th-century Royal Infirmary (which was rebuilt on the site of the earlier building, designed by Robert Adam). The site of the Cathedral has been a place of Christian worship since the ground was blessed for burial in 397 AD by Scotland's first known missionary, St Ninian. The present building is an extension of two earlier churches dedicated in 1136 and 1197, and it was largely completed

Glasgow Cathedral from the Western Necropolis

TO THE MEMORY OF
WILLIAM MILLER
THE LAUREATE OF THE NURSERY
AUTHOR OF WEE WILLIE WINKIE
BORN IN GLASGOW
DIED 20 AUGUST 1872

Cathedral Nave

Cathedral Crypt or Lower Church

in the 13th century, except for the stone quire screen and the Blacader Aisle of the Lower Church, both dating in their present form from the 15th century. At the Reformation considerable damage was done to the furnishings but the building itself remained whole and roofed. Sadly, mid-19th century developments led to the removal of two towers on the western facade.

The building with its soot-darkened stone has a simple almost severe beauty. It contains some very ornate carving, including the large quire screen which almost divides the church in two. Most of the stained glass is of recent Scottish origin, and was installed since the Second World War; but apart from the quire, most of the windows are clear glass. The Lower Church or Crypt dates from the 13th century and is a fine example of early Gothic style; it contains the tomb of St Mungo, a place of pilgrimage in medieval times. The west wall is covered by a beautiful modern Scottish tapestry.

Just to the west of the Cathedral, in front of the Royal Infirmary, is the site of the Bishop's Castle; badly damaged at the Reformation, in spite of 17th-century restoration, it gradually fell into ruin until it became a quarry in 1755. It finally disappeared at the building of the first Royal Infirmary in 1789.

In 1986 work began on an exciting £12 million project to revitalise the precincts of Glasgow Cathedral. This imaginative attempt to enhance the importance of the area as a tourist venue will include extensive landscaping, stonecleaning, construction and a new life for the redundant **Barony Church** on the corner of Castle Street and Macleod Street; a fine example of Gothic Revival style, it will be used by the University of Strathclyde as its main ceremonial hall. The Friends of Glasgow Cathedral plan a visitors' centre which, along with new housing, will recreate the traditional approach to the Cathedral in the form of a 'processional way'.

Behind the Cathedral is the **Western Necropolis**, a Victorian cemetery on a spectacular hilly site, well worth a visit for its ornate tombs, monuments of an age that believed in solidity. It is said to be the first British example of a romantic cemetery on the model of the Père Lachaise Cemetery in Paris. It is capped at its highest point by a statue of Scotland's 16th-century reformer, John Knox

Tombs in the Western Necropolis

(which stood there before the cemetery was laid out). Just outside the gates in Cathedral Square is the former **Barony North Church** (1878) in Italianate style, now the Glasgow Evangelical Church.

From the Cathedral, Castle Street leads south into High Street, on the line of the medieval route between the Cathedral and the lowest crossing point on the Clyde. On the left is the site of the Old College, the fine Renaissance building of Glasgow University, demolished when the University sold out to railway companies in the late 19th century, and moved west (see p. 52). This area contains some excellent sandstone tenements, built in the 1890s by the City Improvement Trust — one of the most enlightened city housing campaigns in Britain at that time. At the foot of High Street is **Glasgow Cross**, centre of the later medieval town. (The earlier centre was further up High Street, where the Drygate met Rottenrow.) Of the 17th-century Tolbooth or Town House there survives only the seven-storey **Tolbooth Steeple**, with its crown tower. The nearby **Mercat Cross** is a 20th-century replacement of one long since demolished.

From the Cross, the Saltmarket takes us to **Glasgow Green**, alongside the River Clyde. Originally the common grazing of the medieval burgh, it is the city's oldest public park, indeed the oldest in Britain, having come into the ownership of the burgh in 1662. For centuries it was a focal

Tolbooth Steeple with start of Glasgow Marathon

People's Palace

point of Glasgow life both for recreation and for meetings of various kinds, being the scene of many political meetings and demonstrations. Recently it has become the finishing point of the Glasgow Marathon, held every autumn. In the centre is the **People's Palace** (see p. 40) and opposite it **Templeton's Carpet Factory** (architect William Leiper), built in 1889 with strong architectural influence from the Doge's Palace in Venice; it has recently been converted into the Templeton Business Centre, with ample space for small offices and workshops, as well as sports and

Templeton's Carpet
Factory (now
Templeton Business
Centre)

Briggait shopping
centre

leisure facilities. To the north-west of the Green are two churches of interest, both in elegant 18th-century style: **St Andrew's Parish Church** (1739-56) in St Andrew's Square contains superb plasterwork (by Thomas Clayton of London) as well as some splendid joinery, said to be made of North American and Caribbean hardwood brought back as ballast in tobacco ships; **St Andrew's-by-the-Green** (1750) in Turnbull Street was Glasgow's oldest Episcopal church until its closure in 1975. A little further north, just off London Road, is **The Barras**, Glasgow's famous weekend market (see p. 64).

Returning to the Saltmarket, we retrace our steps, with the **High Court** on the left; the original Greek Revival building (1807-14, architect William Stark) served as the city chambers until 1844; it was rebuilt in 1910 and only the portico remains of the original building. A little beyond we turn left onto Bridgegate. Near the River, the **Merchants' Steeple**, all that remains of the 17th-century Merchants' House, dominates the old **Fishmarket** (1873). This pleasant building has recently been converted into the **Briggait** shopping centre (see p. 64).

SV Carrick

St Andrew's
Cathedral through
the Suspension
Bridge

We approach the river again at the Victoria Bridge, built in 1854 to replace the Old Glasgow Bridge, which had stood there since the 14th century. Alongside it is moored the SV **Carrick**, an old clipper which is the headquarters of the Royal Naval Volunteer Reserve Club of Scotland. The ship still holds the world sailing record of 65 days for the 12 000 mile voyage from Adelaide, Australia, to London. After recent renovation, this part of the city, on both sides of the river, has a pleasant elegant air, enhanced by the Suspension Bridge for pedestrians, between Victoria Bridge and Glasgow Bridge. The **Custom House Quay**, now part of the Clyde Walkway (see p. 24), takes us past St **Andrew's Roman Catholic Cathedral** (architect James Gillespie Graham); built in 1816, it was one of Glasgow's earliest examples of Gothic Revival Style. We turn right into Jamaica Street, on the west side of which is **Gardner's** (now Martin-Frost's) furniture warehouse, a remarkable and beautifully-proportioned cast-iron structure of 1855-56. Jamaica Street leads to Argyle Street, one of Glasgow's main shopping areas (see p. 63). To the west is the **Central Station** (see p. 70) with its bridge over Argyle Street, known as the **Hielanman's Umbrella**, as it was once a favourite rendez-vous for the many Highlanders who came to live in the city. A little to the east is **St Enoch Square**, once the home of another of Glasgow's mainline railway stations, a victim of the Beeching axe in the 1960s. It still contains the **St Enoch Square Underground Station** (1896), a little gem of toytown architecture, with many interesting details. The building is now a travel centre, adjoining the modern station. A £62 million shopping complex is currently being built in the Square (see p. 63).

Round the corner in Mitchell Street is the former **Glasgow Herald building** (now owned by an insurance company). It was built in 1893-5 to a design from the firm of Honeyman and Keppie, by whom Charles Rennie Mackintosh was employed, then as a draughtsman. His influence is seen in many features, including the proportions of the windows and positioning of the tower.

Hielanman's Umbrella

An alternative route from Clyde Street takes us up Stockwell Street to the junction of Argyle Street and Trongate. The **Tron Steeple**, dating ❹ from the late 16th-early 17th centuries, is all that is left of the Tron Church, burnt down in the late 18th century. The Church was rebuilt behind and it now houses the **Tron Theatre** (see p. 44). From the Trongate, Candleriggs takes us to the **City Hall** (see p. 43). At the

Tron Steeple

junction with Ingram Street is **St David's (Ramshorn) Church** (1824), built on the site of an earlier church whose churchyard contains the graves of many famous Glaswegians, including the 18th-century Foulis brothers, printers and founders of an Academy of Fine Art, and David Dale, a cotton-mill owner who was a pioneer in industrial welfare. To the left along Ingram Street, **Hutchesons' Hospital Hall** ❺ (1802-5, architect David Hamilton) is now the Glasgow home of the National Trust for Scotland. Recently restored, the building has a National Trust Visitor Centre and shop, and is available for recitals, exhibitions etc. Its elegant classical facade contains two 17th-century statues of the Hutcheson brothers, George and Thomas, who founded a hospital for eleven aged men and later for ten orphan boys. The trust which financed the hospital later set up two grammar schools, one for boys and one for girls; still very much in existence, they are now joined into one school.

**Hutchesons'
Hospital Hall**

A little way down from Ingram Street in Glassford Street is ❻ the **Trades House**. Designed by Robert Adam, it was opened in 1794 as the headquarters of the Trades House of Glasgow, a federation of 14 of the city's trade Incorporations. Although it no longer has power in the running of trades, the organisation continues to exist for charitable purposes. In spite of considerable alterations, the building retains the original Adam facade, with single bays added later at each side.

Trades House

From Ingram Street, South Frederick Street leads to George Square. Dominated by its many statues, especially that of Sir Walter Scott on its 80-foot column, it is the centre of modern Glasgow. The east side is completely occupied by the massive **City Chambers** (1883- ♿ 88, architect William Young), now showing its Victorian splendour to full effect after recent stone-cleaning. The marble-clad interior, especially the staircase, is a worthy monument to the opulence of 19th-century Glasgow. There are generally guided tours at 10.30 am and 2.30 pm Monday to Friday or by arrangement. The building is joined to its early 20th-century extension in Cochrane Street by two huge arches. George Square's other reminders of the Victorian era include the **Head Post Office** (see p. 76) on the south side and the **Merchants' House** on the northwest corner. Now the home of the Glasgow Chamber of Commerce, it contains many relics of the city's past as a merchant city, including a gold ship on the top, a replica of one on the original Merchants' House (see p. 23). The rest of that block is occupied by the **Bank of Scotland** on the corner of St Vincent Place; further along on the opposite side is the **Greater Glasgow Tourist Information Centre**. Their helpful and friendly staff will provide information on anything the visitor might need (see also p. 69).

City Chambers (interior)

George Square

Upper view of Stock Exchange House with St George's Tron Steeple

Stirling's Library   Merchants' House

Just behind is **Royal Exchange Square**, completely dominated by **Stirling's Library**. The view of its neoclassical facade from Ingram Street is spectacular, enhanced by the equestrian statue of the Duke of Wellington in front. The building began life as the 18th-century mansion of William Cunningham, one of the 'Tobacco Lords'. In 1817 it became the Glasgow headquarters of the Royal Bank of Scotland. It later became the Royal Exchange, and in 1832 a new building was completed (to the design of David Hamilton), adding a massive portico, a clock tower and a large extension to the original mansion. The library was originally a private foundation set up in 1791 with the aid of a bequest from Walter Stirling, a Glasgow merchant. It became a Glasgow Corporation library in 1912 and moved to its present home in 1954. Two sides of the Square have fine Georgian buildings and at the back is the 1827 **Royal Bank of Scotland** (architect Archibald Elliott), a Grecian-style building flanked by two large archways leading into Royal Bank Place and Buchanan Street. At the corner is Porteous's bookshop, well supplied with maps and guides for the visitor.

Buchanan Street, with its lower part pedestrianised is Glasgow's most elegant, upmarket shopping street (see p. 63). Further up, at Nelson Mandela Place (formerly St George's Place) are several interesting 19th-century buildings. In the centre is **St George's Tron Church** (1807, architect William Stark), with its remarkable classical-baroque steeple. On the bottom corner is the **Glasgow Stock** &. **Exchange House** (1875-77, architect John Burnet), a late example of the Gothic Revival. Behind the church is the **Royal Faculty of Procurators** (1854), a richly ornamented building in Italian Renaissance style. The top corner has three buildings currently occupied by the Royal Scottish Academy of Music and Drama (see p. 54). The early 20th-century red sandstone building at the corner (formerly the Liberal Club) is flanked by two earlier buildings (originally the Athenaeum).

Royal Faculty of Procurators

TOUR OF THE CITY CENTRE (WEST)

From near the top of Buchanan Street, Sauchiehall Street runs in a westerly direction. It is one of Glasgow's principal streets and contains one of its main shopping areas (see p. 63); from West Nile Street to Blythswood Street it is now a pedestrian precinct. The name means 'willow meadow', having been altered from 'Sauchiehaugh'. To the right in Hope Street is the **Theatre Royal** (see p. 44) and beyond it in the Cowcaddens, the headquarters of Scottish Television. On the left, beyond the

Willow Tearoom

Sauchiehall Street Centre (see p. 63), the facade of Charles Rennie Mackintosh's **Willow Tearoom** can still be seen. For many years part of Daly's department store, it is now Henderson's jewellery and gift shop and the Room de Luxe on the first floor has been restored to its former use, with reproduction Mackintosh furniture.

To the right in Rose Street is the **Glasgow Film Theatre** and, a little further along Sauchiehall Street, the **McLellan Galleries**, built in the 1850s by Bailie Archibald MacLellan to house his own private collection. The paintings, initially the subject of some controversy, later became the nucleus of Glasgow's fine civic collection and the building is now used for various exhibitions and functions. Behind it in Renfrew Street is the **Glasgow School of Art**, designed by Charles Rennie Mackintosh and considered to be his masterpiece (see p. 55). A little to the north in Buccleuch Street is the **Tenement House** (see p. 41). At **Charing Cross** Sauchiehall Street crosses the M8 Motorway. Several 19th-century buildings were demolished to make way for it, but the more fantastical architectural ideas of the Victorian age, with French Renaissance influence, survive in **Charing Cross Mansions** (1891), early work

Charing Cross Mansions

of the great Glasgow architect J J Burnet.

On the other side of the motorway bridge is a charming red-sandstone fountain which now stands rather forlornly beside Sauchiehall Street. Further along in North Street is the **Mitchell Library** (see also p. 42), the grandeur of its 1911 building now more clearly seen since the demolition of buildings opposite to make way for the Motorway. In recent years it has extended into the site of the old St Andrews Halls (see p. 43), retaining the original facade and housing the Mitchell Theatre (see p. 44).

St Andrews Hall facade

Mitchell Library at night

**Trinity College
tower**

Park Terrace

Trinity College was built as the Free Church College but has recently been very successfully converted into flats. **Park Circus** (1855), with its curved terraces, is the high point of the area in more than one sense. Its lofty site overlooks Kelvingrove Park and the University of Glasgow to the west, and to the south the Clyde with its dramatic array of cranes and the Renfrewshire hills beyond.

Blythswood Square

North-west of Charing Cross is an area of very elegant Victorian architecture adjoining Kelvingrove Park (see p. 46) on the far side. Though now largely given over to business premises, parts remain residential. The area is dominated by the towers of **Trinity College** (1856-61) and by the remaining tower of **Park Church** (1858), now attached to a modern office block.

Returning to Charing Cross and east along Bath Street, we come to the **King's Theatre** (see p. 44) and a little to the south-east, **Blythswood Square** and its surrounding streets provide another good example of wealthy late Georgian/early Victorian Glasgow. Now almost all offices, the area was once the scene of elegant living. In St Vincent Street, near Pitt Street, is the former **St Vincent Street Church** (1859), designed by Alexander 'Greek' Thomson. Long disused, it is in temporary use by a Free Church congregation and there are plans to convert it into an arts centre. This area of the city contains many imposing commercial buildings which are a reminder of Glasgow's prosperity in the 19th and early 20th century. These include the **Mercantile Chambers** (1897-8) in Bothwell Street, the **'Hatrack'** (1899, architect James Salmon) in St Vincent Street and the **Lion Chambers** (1905, also by Salmon) in Hope Street, Glasgow's earliest concrete commercial building; its outer walls are only about four inches thick.

St Vincent Street Church

'Hatrack'

Lion Chambers

ART GALLERIES AND MUSEUMS

This list covers public, private and commercial galleries. Those run by Glasgow District Council are marked * and information on any of them may be had from the headquarters at the Art Gallery and Museum, Kelvingrove (041) 357 3929.

T & R Annan & Sons 130 West Campbell Street (041) 221 5087, sells a large range of original paintings and also reproductions. It has an excellent collection of old Glasgow photographs.

  *Art Gallery and Museum Kelvingrove G3 (041) 357 3929. Built at the end of last century for the Glasgow International Exhibition of 1901, its paintings form one of the finest municipal collections in Britain, being particularly strong in 17th-century Dutch paintings as well as in 19th-century French paintings of the Barbizon, Impressionist and Post-Impressionist periods.

In the late 19th century painting in the city had a special flowering in the work of the Glasgow School, or the Glasgow Boys as they called themselves. They broke new ground in their departure from rigid academic tradition into a fresh and lively approach. Their paintings are well represented in Kelvingrove, including works by E A Hornel, James Guthrie, E A Walton, George Henry and John Lavery. The adjoining gallery features the work of the Scottish Colourists such as S J Peploe, F C B Cadell, and J D Fergusson.

World-famous paintings in the Gallery include *The Man in Armour* by Rembrandt, The portrait of Thomas Carlyle by Whistler, *Going to Work* by Millet, and *Christ of St John of the Cross* by Dali.

The museum side includes important collections in the fields of natural history, archaeology, ethnography, as well as decorative arts such as ceramics, glass, jewellery and furniture. The strength of Glasgow's contribution to these

Art Gallery and Museum, Kelvingrove

arts around the turn of the century is exhibited in a gallery devoted to the Glasgow Style, with many examples of the design of Charles Rennie Mackintosh and his contemporaries. It includes a reconstruction of part of the Chinese Room of Mackintosh's Ingram Street Tearooms, which were demolished in 1971.

The Museum contains an internationally renowned collection of arms and armour, including Scottish weaponry.

Rembrandt's *Man in Armour*, Kelvingrove

 & *****The Burrell Collection** Pollok Country Park (041) 649 7151. When Sir William Burrell, a wealthy shipowner, gifted his priceless art collection to the city in 1944, his deed of gift specified that a gallery to house the collection should be built at least 16 miles away near Killearn in Stirlingshire, because he feared air pollution in Glasgow might damage many of the priceless items. In 1959 Glasgow began a smoke-control campaign which was to make it one of the cleanest industrial cities in Britain, and in 1967 Mrs Anne Maxwell Macdonald gave to the city the Pollok Estate, only three miles from the centre (see p. 46). The trustees of the Burrell Collection agreed that Pollok was an ideal location for the gallery and it was eventually opened by the Queen in October 1983. It was an immediate success and both the building and its designer have since won many awards.

The Burrell Collection is one of the most varied exhibitions of its size anywhere, including as it does Chinese ceramics, antiquities from the ancient civilisations of the Mediterranean, Persian carpets, medieval stained glass, tapestries and furniture, as well as modern painting and sculpture. With over four million visitors in its first three and a half years, it has proved to be one of Britain's most popular galleries.

Burrell Collection
(exterior)
(interior)

Collins Gallery University of Strathclyde, Richmond Street, G1 (041) 552 4400 ext. 2682/2416. Founded in 1973 as part of the University of Strathclyde, it has about a dozen shows per year covering diverse arts and subjects. In recent years it has paid special attention to photography. It is also used for recitals, poetry readings etc.

Compass Gallery 178 West Regent Street, G2 (041) 221 6370. Set up in 1968 by Cyril Gerber, the gallery concentrates on contemporary art, giving particular encouragement to younger Scottish artists. An annual *New Generation Show* is held to exhibit the best from the four Scottish art schools.

Cyril Gerber Fine Art 148 West Regent Street, G2 (041) 221 3095/ 204 0276. Exhibits largely from its own stock and concentrates on mid and early 20th and late 19th century, with a large share to the Scottish artists of the turn of the century.

The Fine Art Society 134 Blythswood Street, G2 (041) 332 4027. An old-established London gallery which now has two galleries in Scotland, in Glasgow and Edinburgh, it exhibits a wide range of painting, both contemporary and of earlier periods, with a strong emphasis on Scottish art. It also includes decorative arts, with many exhibits of Charles Rennie Mackintosh and his contemporaries.

French Institute see p. 86.

Glasgow Arts Centre 12 Washington Street, G3 (041) 221 4526. Run by Strathclyde Region Education Department, it aims to provide, from its very central location in Anderston, opportunities for participation in and enjoyment of the arts, in the widest sense of the word and to as wide a range of people as possible. Its programmes include classes, workshops, exhibitions and performances.

Glasgow Print Studio 128 Ingram Street, G1 (041) 552 0704. A workshop where printmakers can produce, exhibit and sell their work. As well as showing members' work, it holds a wide variety of other exhibitions.

Glasgow Print
Studio

Goethe-Institut, Glasgow see p. 86.

 & *****Haggs Castle** 100 St Andrews Drive, G41 (041) 427 2725. Originally the 16th-century home of the Maxwells of Pollok, the Castle was restored from its ruined state in the 19th century. In recent years it has been made into a period museum with special emphasis on educational activities for children. The grounds are also of interest historically, with many plants, including herbs, which were in use in former centuries.

Haggs Castle,
schoolchildren in
Museum

Hunterian Museum and Art Gallery & ☞ University of Glasgow (041) 330 4221 (Museum), 330 5431 (Art Gallery). The core of both is in the private collections of the 18th-century anatomist and physician, William Hunter, who left them to the University. The **Museum**, in the University's main building, has important geological and archaeological material, as well as Hunter's remarkable coin collection. The **Art Gallery**, in Hillhead Street, contains, as well as Hunter's collection of paintings, important items from many periods, including numerous Scottish paintings, and one of the largest collections of James MacNeill Whistler in existence. **Mackintosh House** contains reconstructions of rooms from Charles

Rennie Mackintosh's own house in nearby Southpark Avenue, as well as many other examples of his design.

*McLellan Galleries 270 Sauchiehall Street (041) 332 1132 — see p. 30.

Main Fine Art The Studio Gallery, 16 Gibson Street, G12 (041) 334 8858. Specialises in young contemporary Scottish artists.

Whistler's *Red and Black — The Fan,* Hunterian Art Gallery

Metro Gallery 713 Great Western Road, G12 (041) 339 0737. A commercial gallery which holds regular exhibitions and sells limited-edition prints, water colours and work by Scottish artists.

Museum for the 602 (City of Glasgow) Squadron Queen Elizabeth Avenue, Hillington (041) 882 6201 ext. 105. Set up by 2175 Squadron Air Training Corps to commemorate this famous squadron.

*Museum of Transport Glasgow's famous transport museum contained the largest range of vehicles in the UK. It was opened in a disused tram depot in Albert Drive on the south side of the city in 1964. Time took its toll on the building and it was closed in January 1987. It will reopen, even bigger and better, in the spring of 1988 as part of the Kelvin Hall sports and recreation complex (see p. 80).

Glasgow Tram, Museum of Transport

*People's Palace Glasgow Green (041) 554 0223. Built at the turn of the century as a cultural centre for the East End community, it provides a mirror of Glasgow life throughout its history, with special emphasis on the social and industrial life of the people in the 19th century. Its red sandstone building is adjoined by the glass and cast-iron structure of the **Winter Gardens**.

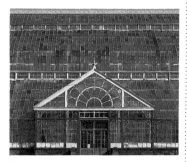

Winter Gardens, People's Palace

***Pollok House** see p. 46.

● ***Provand's Lordship** 3 Castle Street (041) 552 8819 — see p. 18.

Queen's Cross Church 870 Garscube Road, G20 (041) 946 6600. A former church designed by Charles Rennie Mackintosh in the 1890s. In an Art Nouveau/Gothic style, its square tower is influenced by that of the medieval parish church of Merriott in Somerset. In 1977 it became the headquarters of the Charles Rennie Mackintosh Society and it is now in constant use for exhibitions, lectures etc.

& **Royal Highland Fusiliers Museum** 581 Sauchiehall Street (041) 332 5634. Exhibits all kinds of mementos of 300 years of infantry history

— uniforms, weapons, medals, pictures. (The regiment was formed in 1959 by the amalgamation of the Royal Scots Fusiliers and the Highland Light Infantry.)

Scotland Street School Museum of Education (041) 429 1202. Designed by Charles Rennie Mackintosh, this red sandstone building was opened in 1904. It follows the basic school plan of its day, but has many

Queen's Cross Church

Scotland Street School

interesting features, especially the two large glass-encased circular staircases. The school closed in 1979 but the building now houses a Museum of Education, run by Glasgow's Museum Education Service.

&. **Scottish Design Centre** 72 St Vincent Street (041) 221 6121. The Design Council's Centre has constant exhibitions of well-designed goods as well as a shop and coffee area.

🅑 **Tenement House** 145 Buccleuch Street (041) 333 0183. In 1982 the National Trust for Scotland bought a two-room-and-kitchen flat in an 1892 tenement in Garnethill. It had been remarkably well-preserved and the Trust has since restored it and opened it as a museum giving interesting sidelights on the social life of Glasgow around the turn of the century.

Third Eye Centre 350 Sauchiehall &. 🅑 Street (041) 332 7521. A multimedia arts centre opened in 1975, it houses a great variety of exhibitions, with emphasis on modern art. Its small theatre has a very varied programme of plays, music, films, talks, poetry readings etc. It also has a bookshop and a café/bar serving vegetarian food.

Tenement House

LIBRARIES

Glasgow's library service is one of the best in Britain. Its 42 lending libraries issue more than eight million items a year: books, records, cassettes, Braille items, large-print material, talking books for people with impaired sight, and many thousands of audio items for linguistic minorities.

  The **Mitchell Library**, headquarters of Glasgow District Libraries, is the largest civic-owned reference library in Europe. It was originally set up by a bequest by Stephen Mitchell of the Glasgow tobacco firm and it celebrated its centenary in 1977. The library is Scotland's only patent deposit library. Among its many resources is facsimile transmission equipment which enables documents to be sent to other parts of Britain in seconds.

The **Glasgow Room** of the Mitchell contains 20 000 books about the city, directories, parish records, maps, prints, photographs, family papers, diaries, valuation rolls, census returns, and registers of voters. It has 3 500 books printed in Glasgow before 1801. Another department contains material published by the British Government, the United Nations, and the European Economic Community. The Mitchell also incorporates the **Commercial Library** with information on all aspects of business.

Most libraries take current newspapers and magazines, and throughout the city there are books in most European languages, as well as material for Indian, Pakistani, and Chinese communities.

For hours of opening or other information about any of the libraries, please contact: The Mitchell Library, North Street, G3 (041) 221 7030.

Looking inside Stirling's Library (see p. 29)

PERFORMING ARTS, CONCERT HALLS, THEATRES see also p. 83

Glasgow is home to a large number of Scotland's most important music and theatre organisations, including Scottish Opera, the Scottish National Orchestra, BBC Scottish Symphony Orchestra, National Youth Orchestra for Scotland, Scottish Ballet, Scottish Theatre Company, as well as the Royal Scottish Academy of Music and Drama. The city hosts three international festivals, Mayfest, the International Jazz Festival and the International Folk Festival, which together bring drama, music, and dance groups from all over the world. There are numerous other bodies whose work involves either bringing world-famous musicians and artists to Glasgow or encouraging and training Glaswegians to make their own contribution to the world of music.

Scottish National Orchestra in the City Hall

Concert Halls

By 1990 Glasgow will at last have a new concert hall at the top of Buchanan Street to replace the famous St Andrews Halls in Granville Street, burnt down in 1962. The new hall will cost £18 million and will seat 2 500 people (see also p. 63). In the meantime, the **City Hall** in the Candleriggs provides, on a smaller scale, excellent acoustics and a pleasant atmosphere for concert-going. The building also contains Glasgow's **Ticket Centre** (041)

552 5961, a computer-controlled Central Box Office for King's Theatre, Mitchell Theatre and City Hall itself (tel. as above).

Since 1979 the Scottish National Orchestra has had a permanent rehearsal centre in the **Henry Wood Hall**, the former Trinity Church in Claremont Street. &

Theatres

Citizens' Theatre Gorbals Street & ⓲ (041) 429 0022, one of Glasgow's older theatre buildings. Formerly the Princess Theatre in the heart of the Gorbals, it now stands curiously isolated, and its rather bleak setting contrasts with its lavish interior. Since it was founded in 1942 by the playwright James Bridie, the Citizens' has had a regular winter programme of drama (including a family Christmas show). In recent years its innovative productions have given it international recognition.

King's Theatre
(interior)

 ● **King's Theatre** Bath Street (041) 552 5961 (stage door (041) 248 5153), another traditional building, was built in 1904 by Howard and Wyndham and is now run by Glasgow District Council. It is host throughout the year to varied theatrical production, both professional and amateur, including the annual Christmas pantomime, which follows in a long tradition of Scottish comedy theatre. It has occasional productions from London's West End.

 ● **Mitchell Theatre** North Street (041) 552 5961 or (041) 221 3198. This theatre, seating just over 400 people, is situated in the extension to the Mitchell Library (see p. 42).

 ● **Pavilion Theatre** Renfield Street (041) 332 1846 is Glasgow's theatre for light entertainment, pop etc and has a popular pantomime season.

Theatre Royal Hope Street, G2 (041) ● 331 1234. Formerly a general-purpose theatre like the King's, in 1975 it became the home of **Scottish Opera**. This company was formed in 1962 at a time when opera was a rare event in Scotland and there was thought to be no audience for it. Its present popularity is proof that audiences can be attracted by offering international standards of excellence. The winter season usually presents at least nine productions, some new, some revivals and some shared with other companies. Although tours are an important part of its schedule,

Theatre Royal
(interior)

Glasgow remains its base. The theatre is also frequently used by Scottish Ballet, Scottish Theatre Company, National Theatre, Ballet Rambert and other visiting companies and by artists, such as Kiri Te Kanawa, Barbara Dickson, Mike Harding, the Corries.

Third Eye Centre see p. 41.   ●

Tron Theatre 38 Parnie Street, G1 ● (041) 552 4267. The Glasgow Theatre Club, founded in 1979, has provided an excellent small theatre, seating 250 people, within the historic Tron Church (see p. 25).

PUBLIC PARKS AND WALKWAYS

Glasgow is very rich in open space, with over 70 parks, containing varied facilities. Most have bowling greens and many have putting greens, tennis courts and/or football pitches, as well as children's playgrounds and boating ponds. Several have public golf courses (see p. 81).

Bellahouston Park Dumbreck Road, is a pleasant stretch of open ground with a splendid view from its highest point. It was the scene of two memorable events, the Empire Exhibition of 1938 and the visit of Pope John Paul II in 1982. An architectural survivor of the former event is the **Palace of Art** on the northern side, now used as an educational centre. The park also contains one of Glasgow's most popular sports centres as well as a 7-lane running track and facilities for field events.

Botanic Gardens Great Western Road, founded 1817 and on the present site since 1842. As well as being a pleasant public park, with the banks of the River Kelvin as an extension (see p. 51), the Gardens have much of interest to the botanist, in particular collections of orchids and begonias. Of the two large hothouses, the **Kibble Palace** is the more interesting architecturally. It was built originally as a conservatory for the Clyde Coast home of John Kibble, a Glasgow businessman, and was moved to its present site in 1873. Within, white marble statues overlook ornamental ponds.

Kibble Palace (interior)

Glasgow Green see p. 22.

Kelvingrove Park was laid out in the 1850s and it was the scene of major exhibitions in 1888, 1901 and 1911. It is divided by the River Kelvin as it approaches the Clyde and close to the river is the city's main Art Gallery and Museum (see p. 34). On one side the 19th-century building of Glasgow University (see p. 52) towers above it and on the other a steep stairway leads up to some of Glasgow's most elegant Victorian houses in the Park Circus area (see p. 32). The park is scattered with ornamental fountains and statues, including one of Lord Kelvin, who dominated 19th-century science and engineering in Glasgow and beyond, and the extraordinary Stewart Fountain, commemorating the Waterworks Act of 1855 which led to the new water supply from Loch Katrine (see pp. 15, 62). As well as other amenities for children, the park contains a roller-skating rink.

Pollok Park ⁀Pollokshaws Road. With an area of 361 acres of Country Park, it is said to be the largest open space within the boundaries of any city in Europe. Formerly the estate of the Stirling-Maxwells of Pollok, parts of the park have been open to the public since 1911 and by 1967 the whole estate had been gifted to the city by the Maxwell-MacDonald family; the Maxwells had owned it for 700 years. In the centre is **Pollok House**, the splendid 18th-century mansion; though altered internally and extended in the 1890s, it is still furnished in the style of the period. It has a collection of valuable paintings, with an important Spanish element, including some by El Greco, Murillo and Goya, as well as works by Jakob Jordaens, William Blake, Anton Mengs and others. The park contains many interesting plants and a Nature Trail. It is now also the home of the **Burrell Collection** (see p. 37).

Kelvingrove Park, with Glasgow University

Entrance to Pollok
House

Pollok House

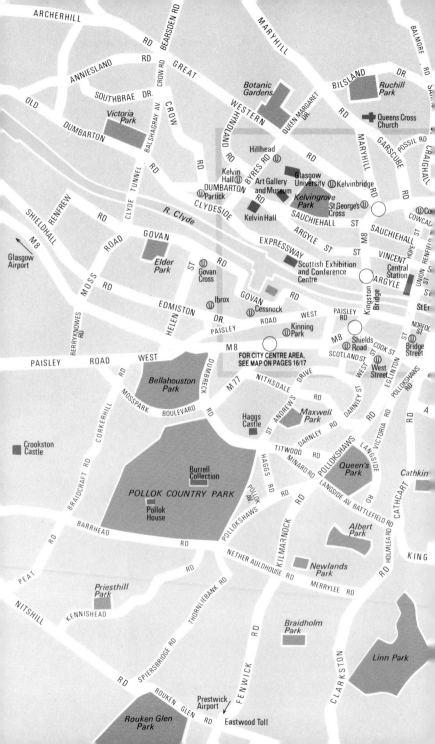

Victoria Park, Victoria Park Drive North, contains Glasgow's most interesting geological exhibition in the **Fossil Grove**. A glasshouse displays several large fossil trees of the Carboniferous period, the era 350 million years ago when coal measures were laid down.

Fossil Grove

In recent years the city has provided several pedestrian routes, especially along the riverbanks, some of them leading out into the countryside. They are part of a broad aim to provide the UK with a network of walks where people can be undisturbed by traffic. Some in Glasgow do indeed provide pleasant peaceful walking only a short distance from sightseeing and shopping areas. The following are now in use:

Clyde Walkway from Stobcross Quay via Glasgow Green (see above), through Dalmarnock to Cambuslang. In the centre, derelict sites along the bank have been cleared to provide landscaped areas, with a bandstand at Custom House Quay.

Suspension Bridge (from Jamaica Bridge)

Kelvin Walkway

Kelvin Walkway from Kelvingrove Park (see p. 46), past Kelvinbridge, through the Botanic Gardens (see p. 45), Wyndford housing scheme, Kelvindale to Dawsholm Park and beyond; the eventual aim is that it should lead right out into the upper reaches of the river and also link up with the West Highland Way (see p. 59).

River Cart Walkway from Corkerhill Road, through Ross Hall and Lochar Parks to Crookston Road.

Levern Walkway about 1 mile from Peat Road Roundabout to Nitshill Road.

Victoria Park Walkway from Westbrae Drive to Dumbarton Road (compensating for part of Victoria Park lost to the approach roads to the Clyde Tunnel).

Brock Burn Walkway along the Brock Burn at Darnley.

The **Forth and Clyde Canal**, which runs from Bowling in the west to Grangemouth in the east, passing through Glasgow, also has stretches of walkway within the city boundary, for example starting at Lock 27, just north of Anniesland Cross (where there is a bar and restaurant).

EDUCATION

This section contains information on Glasgow's two universities and on some of its more important colleges. For information on other educational matters apply to **Strathclyde Regional Council, Education Department** 20 India Street, G2 (041) 204 2900.

The **University of Glasgow** University Avenue, G2 (041) 339 8855, (founded 1451) is the fourth oldest educational institution in the British Isles; along with St Andrews and Aberdeen, it is one of the three Scottish universities founded in the 15th century. Glasgow University was established by Bishop Turnbull and recognised by a Papal Bull of Pope Nicholas V. Predominantly ecclesiastical, it naturally settled in the Cathedral area. In the 17th century, the fine Renaissance building (now referred to as the Old College) was erected in the High Street. It housed the university for 200 years until it was demolished in the 1870s to make way for a railway goods yard. The new building on **Gilmorehill** above Kelvingrove Park was designed by a prominent London architect, Sir George Gilbert Scott, and was opened in 1870. Its Gothic Revival style was continued in the impressive **Memorial Chapel**, designed by Sir John Burnet, which completed the west side of the arts quadrangle in 1928.

Two features of the Renaissance Old College survive: the Lion and Unicorn Staircase next to the Chapel, and Pearce Lodge (now part of Computer Service), which incorporates the Old College's gateway. Both were moved stone by stone to Gilmorehill. Buildings representing various styles of the 20th century include the circular **Reading Room** (1939) and the **Library** (1968).

Halls of residence include converted Victorian terrace houses as well as modern buildings. The most spectacular of the latter is probably Wolfson Hall, set in wooded surroundings in Garscube estate to the west of the city. Garscube is also the site of the University's Veterinary School, which is currently doing important work in cancer and AIDS research, and also of the **West of Scotland Science Park**. This is a project set up jointly by the Universities of Glasgow and Strathclyde, along with the Scottish Development Agency, to forge closer links between science and industry. Companies involved in high technology can set up premises on either of the Park's two sites, Kelvin Campus and Todd Campus, where they can benefit from the ready accessibility of the Universities' research facilities.

Today the University of Glasgow has over 10 000 students in

eight faculties, including Arts, the oldest and largest, and Engineering, the oldest in the world. Among the best-known of its former teachers are Adam Smith, Lord Lister, and Lord Kelvin.

See also **Hunterian Art Gallery and Museum** (p. 38).

Tower of Glasgow University

The **University of Strathclyde** George Street, G1 (041) 552 4400 is one of the oldest technical institutions in the world. In 1795 John Anderson, Professor of Natural Philosophy in the University of Glasgow, left money which helped to found Anderson's Institution. Its name changed many times over the years: in 1912 it became the Royal Technical College and in 1956 the Royal College of Science and Technology; and in 1964 a royal charter made the University of Strathclyde the first new university in Scotland since that of Edinburgh in 1583. It incorporated the Scottish College of Commerce and over the years has widened its base to include a lively faculty of arts and social sciences and the Strathclyde Business School, one of the largest in Europe. But, true to its traditions, it remains first and foremost a technical university with courses in most branches of science and technology. It has over 7 000 students, a considerable number of them from overseas.

The campus is at the heart of the modern city, the oldest building (now known as the Royal College Building) but a stone's throw from the City Chambers. The steep hill rising behind it, where part of medieval Glasgow once stood, provides a spectacular site for its modern buildings. These include several halls of residence; the more distant include **Baird Hall** in Sauchiehall Street, the former Beresford Hotel, a striking example of Art Deco architecture and Beneffrey, an early 20th-century mansion house near Bellahouston Park.

See also **Collins Gallery** (p. 37).

Nearby is the **Glasgow College of Building and Printing** 60 North Hanover Street, G1 (041) 332 9969 and the **Glasgow College of Food Technology** 230 Cathedral Street, G1 (041) 552 3751, both providing

**Baird Hall,
University of
Strathclyde**

specialist education in these subjects. The **Central College of Commerce** 300 Cathedral Street, G1 (041) 552 3941 has courses in Business Studies, Distribution, General Studies, and Hairdressing and Beauty Therapy. Also in the city centre is the **Glasgow College of Technology** 70 Cowcaddens Road, G4 (041) 332 7090, near Buchanan Bus Station. Founded in 1971, if offers a wide range of courses in science and technology as well as some in business studies and social sciences.

The **Royal Scottish Academy of Music and Drama** (041) 332 4101 is the only institution in Scotland specialising in these subjects, with full-time professional courses. Its present site is at the corner of Buchanan Street and Nelson Mandela Place (formerly St George's Place; see p. 29) but is soon to move to modern buildings, designed by Sir Leslie Martin, in Renfrew Street (opposite the Theatre Royal). These will include a large concert hall, as well as theatre space and a TV studio.

Glasgow School of Art 167 Renfrew Street, G3 (041) 332 9797 was founded in 1840. Later in the century its director, Francis Newbery, helped it expand and brought it into prominence internationally. By the 1890s a new building was required and a competition for its design was won by Charles Rennie Mackintosh. The east wing was opened in 1899 but the building of the west wing was held up by financial constraints until 1909. The seminal importance of the building in the Modern Movement in architecture is well known and it remains the finest monument to one of Glasgow's most illustrious sons. Parts of the building are open to the public at certain times; a visit is not to be missed and is best arranged in advance. Its spectacularly steep site gives added effect to Mackintosh's windows, creating a striking place in which to work or study. Mackintosh's furniture can be seen in the library, Director's Room and Board Room (now known as the Mackintosh Room), and the School also has a large collection of Mackintosh's drawings, watercolours and other furniture in the Mackintosh Furniture Gallery.

Glasgow School of Art, exterior

Glasgow College of Nautical Studies 21 Thistle Street, G5 (041) 429 7767. Situated in the Gorbals just south of the Clyde, the College has courses in all aspects of operating ships and shipping. It was formed in the 1960s from several other institutions in the West of Scotland.

Jordanhill College of Education 76 Southbrae Drive, G13 (041) 959 1232. One of Scotland's main institutions for the training of teachers, it has been sited on the west side of the city since 1921.

Queen's College (formerly the Glasgow and West of Scotland College of Domestic Science) 1 Park Drive, G3 (041) 334 8141 is situated on the edge of Kelvingrove Park. The College has a wide variety of courses, including Home Economics, Dietetics, Consumer Studies, Catering and Accommodation Management and Physiotherapy.

Glasgow School of Art, loggia

Glasgow School of
Art, Mackintosh Room

Glasgow School of
Art, entrance

Glasgow School of
Art, staircase

GLASGOW AND ITS SURROUNDINGS

Glasgow is one of the best centres in Britain for visits to a wide variety of spectacular scenery and places of interest. This brief note can do no more than indicate a very few of the many possibilities. The map on pp. 16-17 gives some further idea, and ample information can be had from the **Greater Glasgow Tourist Board Information Centre** (see p. 69).

The city is ideally placed for outdoor sports of all kinds. Some of the best hill-walking and climbing in Britain is within very easy reach, and for those who like less strenuous walks there are delightful loch- and riverside paths and many forest walks. All Scotland's main commercial ski areas are very accessible: Glencoe, Glenshee, Cairngorms; with improved roads even the last is now a reasonable one-day proposition. Sailing on the Firth of Clyde is unsurpassed anywhere and there is also sailing on many inland lochs, notably Loch Lomond. Boating at a more casual level is also available and there are rowing boats for hire for example at Hogganfield Loch. For further information on facilities, see p. 81.

Two of Scotland's traditional industries are whisky and wool, and the visitor may be interested to see these at work. Distilleries near Glasgow which can be visited include:

Auchentoshan, Dalmuir (tel. Duntocher 78561).

Glengoyne, Dumgoyne (tel. Killearn 50254).

Though decreasing in number, there are still woollen mills in the **Borders** and that area is not too distant for a day's excursion.

The outer edges of the city, as well as its near neighbours offer much of interest to the visitor.

Provan Hall, in Auchinlea Park, Garthamlock, some three miles from the centre, off the M8 Motorway, consists of a two-storey 16th-century house, with characteristic round tower and crowstep gables, and an 18th-century house of about the same size. It is built on the site of the medieval manor of the Lords of Provan, whose prebendary occupied Provand's Lordship (see p. 18). The building is on lease from the National Trust for Scotland to Glasgow District Council, and is being converted into a community centre.

Glasgow Zoo, Calderpark, Uddingston (041) 771 1185, six miles south-east of the city centre, is run by the Zoological Society of Glasgow and the West of Scotland, and has a wide variety of species.

Cathcart, on the south side of the city, is a district with strong historical associations. Cathcart Old Parish Church, though a 20th-century building, stands near the ruins of an earlier church, and its churchyard contains tombs dating back to the 17th century.

Greenbank Garden, Flenders Road, Clarkston (041) 639 3281. A garden advice centre is contained within the 16 acres of garden and woodland surrounding an elegant 18th-century house. (The house is not open to the public). There is a garden for the disabled. The property is owned by the National Trust for Scotland.

Crookston Castle

Crookston Castle in the Pollok district, on a ridge above the Levern Water, is a tower house built in the late 14th century by Sir Alexander Stewart, ancestor of the earls of Lennox. It was thus owned by the father of Henry Stewart, Lord Darnley, second husband of Mary, Queen of Scots and they stayed there after their marriage in 1565. Only one of the castle's four square corner towers remains in an almost complete state.

Paisley, seven miles to the west, and to the south of the river, is the largest town bordering on Glasgow. Its history as a burgh goes back to medieval times and it has an abbey of 12th-century foundation, whose Gothic building with square tower can be seen for miles around. It was restored at the turn of the century and is now in use by the Church of Scotland. Nearby is the Place of Paisley ('Place' being a corruption of palace), a group of medieval houses, also restored in recent times. Especially during the Industrial Revolution, Paisley was an important centre of the weaving industry and it became world-famous as the home of the Paisley shawl. A representative collection of these shawls can be seen in the town's excellent Museum and Art Gallery in the High Street.

Paisley Abbey

In the late 19th and early 20th centuries, many Glaswegians holidayed in various resorts on the **Firth of Clyde**, and the journey there was known as going 'Doon the Watter'. These resorts are still accessible by ferry and steamer, including the islands: Arran, the Highlands in miniature, forming a striking contrast with the more agricultural Bute and Cumbrae. There is steamer access from Gourock and from Wemyss Bay, Largs and Ardrossan on the **Ayrshire coast**, Glasgow's most accessible stretch of seaside.

Ayrshire has many reminders of Robert Burns, including **Burns' Cottage** in Alloway. For the golfer, the famous golf links at **Turnberry**, adjacent to one of Scotland's largest hotels, were the scene of the Open Championships in 1977 and 1986. The Open has also been held at Troon and Prestwick. **Culzean Castle**, a huge and splendid 18th-century house designed by Robert Adam, is owned by the National Trust for Scotland. It is set high above the sea coast amid the 563 acres of Scotland's first Country Park.

Adam staircase, Culzean Castle

On the north-west side of the city, the suburb of Bearsden lies on the line of the Antonine Wall, built during the Roman invasion of the 2nd century AD. Sections of Roman road can be seen in·the New Kilpatrick Cemetery and a Roman bath-house was recently excavated during the building of a block of flats in Roman Road.

Roman bathhouse, Bearsden

Mugdock Reservoir, Milngavie

Beyond Bearsden at Milngavie begins the **West Highland Way**, a walkway of about 100 miles to Fort William. It quickly leads out into the countryside on the edges of the Highlands, only a short distance from **Loch Lomond** which well deserves its reputation for some of Scotland's finest scenery.

Loch Lomond

The main access to Loch Lomond from Glasgow is via Great Western Road and this route skirts **Dumbarton** on the Clyde. **Dumbarton Castle**, a medieval fortress, can be seen on its spectacular rock site overlooking the river. The southern end of Loch Lomond is reached at Balloch. At Tarbet, two thirds of the way to its head, two routes into Argyll converge. The road west takes you into popular walking territory, with **Arrochar** at its centre. The road skirts the head of **Loch Long** there, passing the **Cobbler** and surrounding hills and on over the **Rest and be Thankful**, a very steep stretch of road, to Loch Fyne and **Inveraray**, with its famous castle. The road north from Tarbet goes via Crianlarich and Tyndrum, where it forks to **Oban** in the west and **Glencoe** to the north.

An alternative route from Glasgow to the west goes through the seaside town of **Helensburgh**. Charles Rennie Mackintosh's **Hill House** was built here in 1902-04 for the publisher Walter Blackie. Regarded as the finest of Mackintosh's domestic architecture, it is now owned by the National Trust for Scotland and is open to the public.

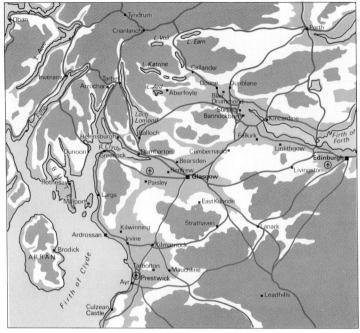

CENTRAL SCOTLAND MAP

Interior of Hill House, Helensburgh

Loch Voil

East of Loch Lomond is the **Tros-sachs**, between Aberfoyle and Callander, a beautiful area of lochs, hills and woods, made popular as an early tourist attraction by Sir Walter Scott in *Rob Roy* and *The Lady of the Lake*. **Loch Katrine** has been a major source of Glasgow's water supply for over a century (see p. 15).

Stirling, 'the Gateway to the Highlands', is less than an hour by train or motorway (M80). Its imposing castle on the rock was an important focal point in medieval Scotland. The magnificent royal palace within the Castle and the old town clustered round it have both been recently restored. Stirling is the home of one of Scotland's new universities, founded in 1967.

Edinburgh, Scotland's capital, lies 45 miles to the east; a journey of under an hour by train, or little more by motorway (M8) takes you to its compact centre, where much can be seen even on a short visit.

Stirling Castle

SHOPPING

Glasgow is the shopping centre of west central Scotland, serving half the country's population. Three of the best-known streets, Buchanan, Argyle and Sauchiehall, are partly pedestrianised. Shopping standards are metropolitan, with local specialist and independent stores alongside Britain's largest multiples, including Marks & Spencer, British Home Stores, C & A, Habitat, Liberty, Jaeger, Dunns, Burton, Austin Reed, Dorothy Perkins and many others. Prices are reasonable enough to attract shopping expeditions from Norway, Sweden, Iceland, France, Belgium and Holland.

Sauchiehall Street's pedestrian area contains the **Sauchiehall Street Centre,** with small and medium-sized units, and there are two other covered-in shopping areas nearby, the **Savoy Centre** almost opposite and the **Cambridge Arcade** in Cambridge Street. Both of these contain amusement arcades.

Buchanan Street has long been Glasgow's most upmarket shopping street, as can be seen in the interior of Fraser's large store, still in the opulent style of an earlier age. Further up is The Highland House of Lawrie, the well-known bagpipe and Highland dress shop. At the top, on the corner of Sauchiehall Street, a £70 million shopping complex is planned to be completed by 1990. It will incorporate a new concert hall to seat 2 500 (see p. 43).

Argyle Street contains in Lewis's Scotland's largest and oldest department store. The street is linked to Buchanan Street by the

Argyll Arcade (1828), an L-shaped covered shopping mall with a variety of small shops, mainly jewellers. Glasgow's main bookstore, John Smith's, is at 57 St Vincent Street, within easy reach of both Queen Street and Central Stations. Work has begun on a £62 million glass-covered complex in St Enoch Square which will be completed in 1989. It will contain 50 shop units, an ice rink, fast-food court, and multi-storey parking for 750 cars. According to the Scottish Development Agency, Glasgow's city centre attracts an annual £2 000 million in retail trade. They believe the new St Enoch development could increase this by another £67 million.

A £40 million shopping development is planned for the site of the old Parkhead Forge, where once the clamour of heavy industry reverberated round the world; it will include the largest Fine Fare store in Britain.

There are lively shopping areas around the edges of the city centre, for example at **Shawlands Cross** on the south and in **Byres Road** and **Dumbarton Road** to the west, as well as in numerous districts further out. The city is well endowed with antique shops and recent enthusiasm for Victoriana has produced in the **Victorian Village** an interesting collection of small shops, forming a Victorian street in former business premises at 53-57 West Regent Street. **The**

Virginia Antique and Craft Galleries, a collection of shops with tearoom, at 31 Virginia Street are located in the old Tobacco Market where auctions were held to sell the shipments newly arrived from America.

Glasgow's most individual shopping experience is undoubtedly **The Barras,** the weekend bargain market in the East End between London Road and the Gallowgate. Covered in since the 1920s, the site has recently been improved, with new facilities such as pedestrian precincts and carparks. (Developments include the reopening of the famous Barrowland Ballroom, now the Barrowland Magic Nite Spot.) Round the corner in Clyde Street the old Fishmarket has recently been converted into the **Briggait Centre,** an indoor shopping complex containing small shops, cafés, and space for informal public entertainment.

There follows a classified list of where to buy what in Glasgow, giving a brief selection of the many possibilities in the city.

antiques

The Bath Street Antique Galleries 203 Bath Street G2 *(041) 248 4396* and *248 4229* 14 shops under one roof.

De Courcys Antique Craft Arcade 5-21 Cresswell Lane G12 *(041) 334 6673* Collection of shops, with tearoom.

Jean Megahy Antiques 481 Great Western Road G12 *(041) 334 1315*

Mercat Antiques 246 West George Street G2 *(041) 204 0851*

Muirhead Moffat & Co 182 West Regent Street G4 *(041) 226 4683/3406*

The Victorian Village 53/57 West Regent Street G2 *(041) 332 0703*

Virginia Antiques & Craft Galleries 31 Virginia Street G1 *(041) 552 2573* see above.

Tim Wright Antiques 147 Bath Street G2 *(041) 221 0364*

auctioneers

J A Cathcart 7 West George Street G2 *(041) 248 6939*

Christie's Scotland 164/166 Bath Street G2 *(041) 332 8134*

Robert McTear & Co Royal Exchange Salerooms St Vincent Place G1 *(041) 221 4456*

Philips 207 Bath Street G2 *(041) 332 3386*

Sotheby's 146 West Regent Street G2 *(041) 221 4817*

audio equipment

Dickson's 121 Byres Road G11 *(041) 334 0430;* 15/17 Queen Street G1 *(041) 204 0826;* 87 Renfield Street G2 *(041) 332 0556;* 62 Woodlands Road G3 *(041) 332 9717*

Hi-Fi Corner 52 Gordon Street G2 *(041) 248 2840*

E W Hutchison 492 Crow Road G11 *(041) 339 7242;* 273 Sauchiehall Street G2 *(041) 332 8676*

James Kerr & Co Ltd 98 Woodlands Road G3 *(041) 332 0988*

Tandy Corporation 223 Ingram Street G1 *(041) 221 9378;* 72 Renfield Street G2 *(041) 333 9608*

bagpipes

James C Begg 62 Robertson Street G2 *(041) 248 4161*

R G Hardie and P Henderson Ltd 24 Renfrew Street G2 *(041) 332 3021*

Kintail of Loch Lomond Ltd 48 Oswald Street G1 *(041) 221 1215*

R G Lawrie Ltd The Highland House of Lawrie 110 Buchanan Street G1 *(041) 221 0217*

books

Bargain Books 89 Byres Road G12 *(041) 339 8184;* 202 Sauchiehall Street G2 *(041) 332 5518*

Church of Scotland Bookshop 160 Buchanan Street G1 *(041) 332 9431*

Crosshill Asian Bookshop
177 Allison Street G42
(041) 423 9440

Frasers
21 Buchanan Street G1
(041) 221 3880

Gairm (Gaelic Bookshop)
29 Waterloo Street G2
(041) 221 1971

Hatchards
50 Gordon Street G1
(041) 221 0262/1780

Hope Street Book Centre
321 Hope Street G2
(041) 332 8881

John Menzies PLC
36-38 Argyle Street G2
(041) 204 0636;
Sauchiehall Street Centre
177 Sauchiehall Street G2
(041) 331 2833

New Glasgow Society
1307 Argyle Street G3
(041) 334 0202 books on
Glasgow.

Pickering & Inglis
26 Bothwell Street G2
(041) 221 8913
(incorporating the Chapter
House Coffee Shop)

William Porteous & Co Ltd
9 Royal Exchange Place G2
(041) 221 8623
has a wide selection of
maps and guide books.

St Paul Book Centre
5a-7 Royal Exchange
Square G1 *(041) 226 3391*

John Smith & Son
(Glasgow) Ltd
57 St Vincent Street G2
(041) 221 7472;
252 Byres Road G12
(041) 221 7472;
John Macintyre Building,
University of Glasgow G12
(041) 339 1463

W H Smith & Son Ltd
53 Argyle Street G2
(041) 221 6061

Third Eye Centre see p. 41

Thistle Bookshops Ltd
6 Havelock Street G11
(041) 334 1085;

John Wylie
406 Sauchiehall Street G2
(041) 332 6177

antiquarian books

Caledonia Bookshop
483 Great Western Road G12
(041) 334 9663

Cooper Hay
203 Bath Street G2
(041) 226 3074

Voltaire & Rousseau
12-14 Otago Lane G12
(041) 339 1811

camping equipment
see **sports**

chemists For late opening
chemists, see p. 78

There are Boots branches
and others around the city
centre, including Boots at
Central Station
(041) 221 7107 and
McEwans at Queen Street
Station *(041) 332 5870*

clothing

In addition to department
stores (see below) and
chains such as Wallis,
Paige, Austin Reed and
Burton, there are
independent stores, eg:
For women: Roberta Buchan
176 Hope Street G2
(041) 332 6060;
681 Great Western Road G12
(041) 357 2646

For men: A A Carswell
25 Renfield Street G2
(041) 248 7571

department and large stores

Arnotts
193 Argyle Street G2
(041) 248 2951

Bremner & Co Ltd
44 Glassford Street G1
(041) 552 3444

British Home Stores
67 Sauchiehall Street G2
(041) 332 0401

C & A
218 Sauchiehall Street G2
(041) 333 9441;
127 Trongate G1
(041) 552 5191

Frasers
21 Buchanan Street G1
(041) 221 3880

A Goldberg & Sons PLC
21 Candleriggs G1
(041) 552 4959

Habitat
140 Bothwell Street G2
(041) 221 5848

Lewis's Ltd
Argyle Street G2
(041) 221 9820

Marks and Spencer PLC
12 Argyle Street G1
(041) 552 4546;
172 Sauchiehall Street G2
(041) 332 6097

John Menzies PLC
38 Argyle Street G2
(041) 204 0636;
Sauchiehall Street Centre
177 Sauchiehall Street G2
(041) 331 2833

Mothercare Ltd
58 Union Street G1
(041) 248 3629

Watt Bros
119 Sauchiehall Street G2
(041) 332 5831

F W Woolworth & Co Ltd
300 Byres Road G12
(041) 339 1501;
412 Dumbarton Road G11
(041) 339 4623

dry cleaners

Pullars of Perth
492 Sauchiehall Street G2
(041) 332 2186

Swiss Cleaners
164a Buchanan Street G2
(041) 332 3396

flowers

Micheleen
456 Duke Street G1
(041) 556 1555;
84 Mitchell Street G1
(041) 226 3004;
21-23 Queen Street G1
(041) 204 0813 Interflora.

Studio Four
80 West Nile Street G2
(041) 332 7669 Interflora.

gifts

Design Centre
72 St Vincent Street G2
(041) 221 6121

Glasgow City Chambers
Gift Shop City Chambers
George Square G2
(041) 227 4627
(front door reception)
Open 10am-4pm Mon-Fri.

National Trust
Hutcheson's Hall
158 Ingram Street G2
(041) 552 8391
Mon-Sat 10am-4pm

Norway House
111 West George Street G2
(041) 248 7888

Post Shop (GPO)
87-91 Bothwell Street G2
Open Mon-Fri 8:30am-
5:30pm; Saturday 9am-
12:30pm for purchase of
stamps, post cards, coin
sets and stationery.

Robin Hood Gift House Ltd
11 St Vincent Place G1
(041) 221 7408

hairdressers

Cut and Dried
118 Sauchiehall Street G2
(041) 332 0066

Harold Kramer
65 Queen Street G1
(041) 248 4008;
87 Queen Street G1
(041) 221 7574;
62 Union Street G1
(041) 204 2424

Irvine Rusk
49 West Nile Street G1
(041) 221 1472

Sweeney Todds
27a St Vincent Place G1
(041) 221 4321

ironmongers

Crocket the Ironmongers
Ltd 136-142 West Nile
Street G1
(041) 332 1041

McFarlane (Trongate) Ltd
16 Trongate G1
(041) 552 0710

John McMillan & Son
87 Saltmarket G1
(041) 552 4265

jewellery

Argyll Arcade G1 (between
Argyle Street and Buchanan
Street) G1 has many
jewellers shops under one
roof, for example H Samuel.

Henderson
217 Sauchiehall Street G2
(041) 331 2569

Laing
26a Renfield Street G2
(041) 221 0121

Mappin & Webb
67 St Vincent Street G2
(041) 221 7683

knitwear and sheepskin coats

Antartex Ltd
127 Buchanan Street G1
(041) 204 1167
Sheepskin coats

Henry Burton & Co Ltd
111 Buchanan Street G1
(041) 221 7380

Clan Royal of Scotland Ltd
137 Buchanan Street G1
(041) 221 1929

The Edinburgh Woollen
Mill 75 Nelson Mandela
Place G1 (formerly
St George's Place)
(041) 221 2252

R G Lawrie Ltd The
Highland House of Lawrie
110 Buchanan Street G1
(041) 221 0217

Pitlochry Knitwear Co Ltd
130 Buchanan Street G1
(041) 221 3434

Scotch House
87 Buchanan Street G1
(041) 221 5128

Many shops selling knitting
wool also sell hand-knitted
knitwear.

maps and charts

see also **sports goods** and
bookshops (especially
William Porteous and John
Smith)

Kelvin Hughes
375 West George Street G2
(041) 221 5452 Enter by
Holland Street.

music

Biggars Music at
Hutchison's
273 Sauchiehall Street G2
(041) 332 8676 Rear shop
and basement have
instruments and sheet
music.

The Fiddle Shop
De Courceys Arcade
Cresswell Lane G12
(041) 334 6673 sale and
repair.

McCormacks Music Ltd
33 Bath Street G2
(041) 332 6644 Wide range
of instruments, keyboards.
Pop sheet music.

William Thomson & Sons
97 West George Street G2
(041) 248 6516 Wide range
of instruments, keyboards
and sheet music.

For bagpipe music see
bagpipes p. 64.

opticians

Contact Lens Centre
(Glasgow) Ltd
113 Hope Street G2
(041) 221 2770

Dollond & Aitchison
(Scotland) Ltd
23 West Nile Street G1
(041) 221 9093;
133 Wellington Street G2
(041) 248 5402

Lizars Ltd
101 Buchanan Street G1
(041) 221 8062;
381 Sauchiehall Street G2
(041) 332 3453

photocopying

Copies
156 Buchanan Street G1
(041) 332 7122 Mon-Fri
8:45am-5:30pm Saturday
9:30am-4pm (24 hour
service if in before 1pm)

Prontaprint
9 Bothwell Street G2
(041) 221 3615;
988 Pollokshaws Road G41
(041) 649 5587 Mon-Fri
9am-5:15pm; Saturday
10am-3pm

Rank Xerox Copy Bureau
166 Hope Street G2
(041) 333 0551/2/3

Sprint Print
121 Douglas Street G2 and
531 Sauchiehall Street G2
(041) 333 9393

photographic equipment

Tom Dickson Cameras
121 Byres Road G12
(041) 334 0430;
15-17 Queen Street G1
(041) 204 0826;
87 Renfield Street G2
(041) 332 0556;
62 Woodlands Road G3
(041) 332 9717

Dixons 48 Argyle Street G1
(041) 221 8828;
38 Sauchiehall Street G2
(041) 332 7611;
115 Union Street G1
(041) 248 5711

Jessops Photo Centre
167 Hope Street G2
(041) 248 2457

G E Williamson
(Photographics) Ltd
540 Sauchiehall Street G2
(041) 332 3381

photographic processors

B & S Colour Labs
57 Eliot Street G3
(Finnieston) *(041) 221 8283*
Colour transparencies two
hours for unmounted and
24 hours for mounted.
Colour prints 24 hours.

Clyde Colour Labs
113 West Regent Street G2
(041) 221 5040
Colour transparencies two
hours for unmounted and
24 hours for mounted.
Colour prints 24 hours.

Foto Machine
63 Renfield Street G2
(041) 331 1090
Two-hour service for spool
and disc film.

Many chemists, dry
cleaners, key cutting/shoe
repair shops and petrol
stations have a 24-hour
photo-processing service for
spools and discs (not
transparencies).

records and cassettes

Casa Cassettes
325 Sauchiehall Street G2
(041) 332 1127

The HMV Shop
72 Union Street G1
(041) 221 1850

Virgin Records and Tapes
28-32 Union Street G1
(041) 221 0103

shoes

as well as numerous chains
there are independent
shops such as:

J Allan & Sons Ltd
122 Buchanan Street G1
(041) 204 0114

Romika
14 Royal Exchange Square G1
(041) 248 3743

shoe repairs

L Archibald
138 Byres Road G12

Automagic Heel Bar
109 Buchanan Street G1
(041) 221 0453

City Heel Bar
164 Buchanan Street G1

Makos Shoe Repairs
992 Maryhill Road G20
(041) 946 8146

sports goods

Blacks Camping and
Leisure
132 St Vincent Street G2
(041) 221 4007

Dales Cycles
150 Dobies Loan G4
(041) 332 3406

John Dickson & Sons
20 Royal Exchange Square G1
(041) 221 6794 fishing,
guns.

Duncan Yacht Chandlers
7 Scotland Street G5
(041) 429 6044

Greaves Sports
23 Gordon Street G1
(041) 221 4531

Highrange Sports
200 Great Western Road G4
(041) 332 5533 climbing,
canoes, skiing, camping.

Lumleys
80 Sauchiehall Street G2
(041) 332 2701

Millets
Sauchiehall Street Centre
Sauchiehall Street G2
(041) 332 5617;
71 Union Street G1
(041) 221 1678 climbing,
camping.

Nevisport
261 Sauchiehall Street G2
(041) 332 4814 climbing,
skiing, camping.

Robin Hood Golf Centre
521 Great Western Road G12
(041) 334 4504

The Scout Shop Camping
& Outdoor Centre
21 Elmbank Street G2
(041) 248 5941

Graham Tiso
129 Buchanan Street G1
(041) 248 4877 climbing,
camping

stamps

Buchanan Street Stamps
205 Buchanan Street (1 up) G1
(041) 333 9724

The Glasgow Stamp Shop
7 Scott Street G3
(041) 332 5100

Post Office Philatelic Bureau
George Square G2
(041) 248 2882

Stamp Shop
Victorian Village 53-57
West Regent Street G2
(041) 332 0703

tartan and highland dress

Event Formal Menswear
164a Buchanan Street G1
(041) 332 5088 sale and hire

Frasers
21 Buchanan Street G1
(041) 221 3880 hire with
ex-hire in occasional sales.

R G Lawrie Ltd
The Highland House of Lawrie
110 Buchanan Street G1
(041) 221 0217 sale, no hire.

Moss Bros at Carswell's
25 Renfield Street G2
(041) 226 4241 hire.

Hector Russell Kiltmaker
85 Renfield Street G2
(041) 332 4102 sale and
hire.

Young's Formal Wear
55 Queen Street G1
(041) 221 4080 sale and
hire.

Many of the large hotels in
the city sell tartan and
Highland dress in the hotel
gift shops.

toys and games

Dunns Models
3 West Nile Street G2
(041) 221 0484

Early Learning Centre
93 Mitchell Street G2
(041) 248 2589

Strathclyde Hobby Centre
25 Parnie Street G1

Tam Shepherd's Trick Shop
33 Queen Street G1
(041) 221 2310

video equipment

Tom Dickson Cameras
121 Byres Road G12
(041) 334 0430;
15-17 Queen Street G1
(041) 204 0826;
87 Renfield Street G2
(041) 332 0556;
62 Woodlands Road G3
(041) 332 9717

Hi-Fi Corner Ltd
52 Gordon Street G2
(041) 248 2840

E W Hutchison Ltd
496 Crow Road G11
(041) 339 7242;
273 Sauchiehall Street G2
(041) 332 8676

Video cassettes for hire are
available from video
libraries, centres or clubs
throughout the city.

TRANSPORT, TRAVEL, TOURISM

useful addresses and
telephone numbers

**Greater Glasgow Tourist
Board Information Centre**
35 St Vincent Place G1
(041) 227 4880
(Hours: [*June-Sep*] Mon-Sat
9am-9pm, Sun 10am-6pm
[*Oct-May*] Mon-Sat 9am-
5pm)

**St Enoch Square Travel
Centre**
(041) 226 4826
for all local bus and rail
travel information

British Rail
(041) 204 2844

Passport Office
131 West Nile Street G2
(041) 332 0271

Immigration Office
Administration Block D
Argyll Avenue
Glasgow Airport
(041) 887 4115

tourism

The **Greater Glasgow
Tourist Board** was set up in
1983 to cater for the large
number of tourists from all
over the world who had
come to recognise Glasgow
and its immediate environs
as places well worth a visit.
The current member
authorities of the Board are
Glasgow, Renfrew,
Monklands, Strathkelvin,
and Inverclyde, and its
headquarters are at the
address listed above. There
is also a Tourist
Information Centre in
Paisley.

tourist guides/services
(see also bus tours below)
**British Telecom/GGTB dial
a what's on service**
(041) 248 4000

Scottish Tourist Guides Association
Reservations Secretary
Mrs S Buchanan
2 Ashton Green
East Kilbride G74
(03552) 38094

Videotours
R J McCorrisken
4 George Street
Barrhead G78
(041) 881 9302

road

Glasgow's main-road system has been considerably upgraded in recent years. The M8 Motorway from Edinburgh now passes around the northern and western edges of the city centre and over the Clyde at the Kingston Bridge to link up with Glasgow Airport and the Clyde coast. The crossing of the Clyde at a more westerly point was facilitated in the early 1960s by the Clyde Tunnel, with approaches linking to the M8 to the south and the Clyde Expressway to the city centre on the north. A few miles further west the Erskine Bridge provides a further crossing (with a toll charge of 30p per car).

There is an extensive network of bus routes and long(er)-distance routes terminate at **Buchanan Bus Station** *(041) 332 7133/9191* for the north, north-west and east routes, and at **Anderston Bus Station** *(041) 248 7432* in Argyle Street for the more southerly. (See also **air** below.) Since deregulation of bus services in 1986, it is difficult to give precise information, but for further details, telephone the bus stations or **St Enoch Square Travel Centre** *(041) 226 4826.*

bus companies

Central Scottish
Motherwell *(60 from Glasgow)* 63575

Clydeside Scottish Omnibuses Ltd
4 Gordon Street Paisley
(041) 889 3191

Cotters Coachline
12 Crimea Street G2
(041) 221 8042

Discovering Glasgow Coach Tours
Alex Pringle Coaches
62 Henderland Road
Bearsden G61
(041) 942 6453

John Donnelly
J & E Coaches
4 Kirkhill Terrace
Cambuslang G71
(041) 641 7932

Graham's Bus Service
142 Hawkhead Road Paisley
(041) 887 3831

Kelvin Scottish
Bishopbriggs *(041) 762 0404*

Midland Scottish
Falkirk *(0324) 23985*

Scottish Citylink Coaches
Buchanan Bus Station G2
(041) 332 9644

Skyeways Express Coaches
Ferry Pier Kyle of Lochalsh
(0599) 4328 (buses to Skye)

Southern Coaches
Lochlibo Road Barrhead
Renfrewshire *(041) 881 1147*

Strathclyde's Buses
Larkfield Garage
Victoria Road
(041) 423 6600

Weirs Tours
1361 Dumbarton Road G14
(041) 959 2062

Western Scottish
Kilmarnock *(0563) 22551*

rail see map on p. 71.

Passenger enquiries
(041) 204 2844 (24-hour)

An integrated rail system now links stations for long-distance and local routes, as well as those of the Underground. The city centre has two mainline termini.

&**Central Station** in Gordon Street serves the more southerly routes, including most of the trains to London; the running time of these is now reduced to under 5½ hours. There are connections to the Clyde coast ports (see p. 72) and to the Stranraer-Larne ferry to Northern Ireland. Central is linked by a minibus service to

&**Queen Street Station,** only a few minutes away, with its main entrance in George Square. Queen Street has a half-hourly service to Edinburgh, as well as regular trains to Perth and Stirling, Fife, Dundee and Aberdeen and on the main Highland routes to Inverness, Oban, and Mallaig (the West Highland Railway). Both stations have suburban electric trains running through their low levels, linking the centre to most parts of the city's edge, and including routes to Loch Lomond, Paisley and the Clyde coast.

The **Glasgow Underground,** with its fifteen stations (see map on p. 71), provides a fast circular route around the periphery of the city centre. From its inauguration in 1896 it ran the original rolling stock until the 1970s when it was completely modernised. Its new orange carriages lacked the period charm of their predecessors and the renovated system quickly became known as the Clockwork Orange.

≷ Interchange with British Rail

Ⓤ Interchange with Underground

≡ Travelator link

🛳 Interchange with Caledonian MacBrayne

✈ Prestwick Airport. Bus: Prestwick Station — Airport Terminal

✈ Glasgow Airport. Bus { Central Station (Argyle Street — North Entrance)
Queen Street Station (North Hanover Street)
Anderston and Buchanan Bus Stations

🚌 Inter-terminal bus link

🚌 Bus Route Adjacent to Station

🚐 Park and ride

Ⓟ Parking available

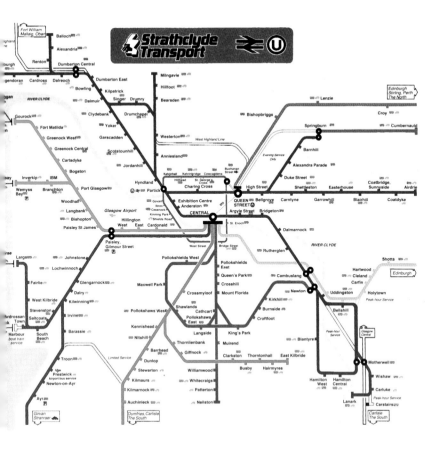

air

&Glasgow Airport
(041) 887 1111, west of
the city at Abbotsinch, is
only 15 minutes drive
from the city centre via
the M8 Motorway. It has
established a reputation
for providing one of the
most advanced and
efficient services in the
UK. In recent years it has
attracted more
international traffic,
including regular flights
and many holiday
charters to Europe and
beyond. The three major
airlines provide an
excellent hourly service
to London Heathrow and
Gatwick, and there are
frequent flights to
complete the UK network.

&Prestwick Airport
(0292) 79822 on the
Clyde coast has
scheduled and charter
flights to North America.
It is Britain's most fog-
free airport and is less
than an hour's drive from
Glasgow. There is an
electric train service to
Central Station, with
connecting minibus from
the airport to Prestwick
Station.

Both airports are
connected to the city
centre by a quick and
efficient bus service,
covering both main rail
and bus stations. The
Glasgow Airport bus also
calls at the Scottish
Exhibition and
Conference Centre.

air charter
Malinair Ltd,
Administration Block A,
Glasgow Airport
(041) 887 1151

helicopter charter
Burnthills Highland
Helicopter Service,
Glasgow Airport
(041) 887 7733

river, sea and loch

Much of Glasgow's wealth
in the past stemmed from
sea traffic on the Clyde and
at one time many ships
sailed from the Broomielaw
to Ireland and the New
World, as well as to towns
on the west of Scotland,
especially the Firth of
Clyde (see p. 59). Now only
two passenger ships run
from Glasgow, the
Waverley, the last seagoing
paddle steamer in the
world, and the *Balmoral*,
with trips from Anderston
Quay during the tourist
season. Further information
from **Waverley Excursions**
(Clyde Steamer Service)
New Waverley Terminal,
Anderston Quay G3 *(041)
221 8152*.

There are also summer
excursion sailings on Loch
Lomond (the *Countess
Fiona*: phone Alloa Brewery
Co *(041) 226 4271* or, for
information only *(041) 248
2699*) and on Loch Katrine
(the *Sir Walter Scott*: phone
Strathclyde Regional
Council Water Department
(041) 336 5333)

steamer and car ferry services
British Rail Sealink Ferries
General Enquiries Central
Station G1 *(041) 204 2844*

Caledonian MacBrayne Ltd
(Clyde Coast and Western
Isles) Ferry Terminal
Gourock *(0475) 33755*

Sealink (Scotland) Ltd
(Stranraer/Larne) Stranraer
Harbour *(0776) 2262*

Townsend Thoresen
The Docks Cairnryan near
Stranraer *(05812) 276*

taxis

**Taxi Cab Association (Radio
Taxis Ltd)**
451 Lawmoor Street G5
(041) 332 6666,
(office) *429 2900*

Taxi Owners Association
6A Lynedoch Street G3
(041) 332 7070,
(office) *332 0054*

The Tourist Information
Centre in St Vincent Place
has a freephone taxi
service.

chauffeur drive

Cowans Chauffeur Service
30 Woodlands Drive G4
(041) 334 9628

Little's Chauffeur Drive
1282 Paisley Road West
G52 *(041) 883 2111*

**H Winchcole Chauffeur
Drive**
214-218 Howard Street G1
(041) 552 0251

car hire

Arnold Clark
St George's Road G3
(041) 332 2626

Avis Rent-A-Car Ltd
161 North Street G3
(041) 221 2827

Budget Rent-A-Car
101 Waterloo Street G2
(041) 226 4141

Callanders Car Rental
1057 Great Western Road
G12 *(041) 334 4646*

Central Rent-A-Car
Elmbank Street G2
(041) 248 6285

Godfrey Davis (Car Hire) Ltd
Queen Street Station G1
(041) 332 7635

Hertz Rent-A-Car
106 Waterloo Street G2
(041) 248 7733

Mitchells Self Drive
Mitchell Street G1
(041) 221 8461

SMT
127 Finnieston Street G3
(041) 204 2828

Swan National Car Hire
222 Broomielaw G1
(041) 204 1051

Universal Garage
367 Alexandra Parade G31
(041) 554 5174

car parks

Car parking in the central area of the city is controlled by parking meters. There are British Rail Car Parks at Central and Queen Street Stations open 24 hours. There are also a number of multi-storey and surface car parks, for example in George Street, Mitchell Street, Waterloo Street, Elmbank Street, Anderston Cross, and Cowcaddens. These are controlled by National Car Parks Ltd, George Street G1 *(041) 552 3150.*

For locations of these and other car parks, see map on p. 16. The following streets in the city centre have spaces reserved for disabled driver permit holders:

Cambridge Street, Miller Street, Pitt Street, Nelson Mandela Place, St Vincent Place.

motoring organisations

Automobile Association
24-hour Breakdown and
Information Service
(041) 812 0101
    Regional Headquarters
Fanum House, Erskine
Harbour, Erskine
(041) 812 0144

Royal Automobile Club
24-hour Breakdown and
Information Service
(041) 248 5474
    General Inquiries 242
West George Street G2
(041) 248 4444

petrol stations with 24-hour service

Alexandra Parade Service Station
367 Alexandra Parade G31
(East of Glasgow Royal Infirmary) *(041) 554 5171*

Arlington Service Station
88 Woodlands Road G3
(Charing Cross)
(041) 333 0510

Broomielaw Auto Point
222 Broomielaw G1 (2 blocks south of the Holiday Inn) *(041) 204 1051*

Callender's West End Service Station
1057 Great Western Road
G12 (at Gartnavel General Hospital) *(041) 334 2708*

Craigpark Service Station
432 Alexandra Parade G31
(East of Glasgow Royal Infirmary) *(041) 554 1302*

Eglinton Service Station
200 Eglinton St G5
(041) 429 3921

Kelvin Service Station
2 Old Dumbarton Road G3
(near Kelvin Hall)
(041) 339 8057

Phoenix Filling Station
431 Keppochhill Road G21
(041) 333 0119

Queen Margaret Drive Self Service Station
162 Queen Margaret Drive
G12 *(041) 945 3754*

St George's Self Service Station
147 St George's Road G3
(Charing Cross)
(041) 332 8773

USEFUL INFORMATION

LOST PROPERTY

Strathclyde buses/Glasgow underground
St Enoch Lost Property Office at St Enoch Underground Station
(041) 248 6950
Mon-Fri 9am-4:45pm

other buses
lost property is sent to the garage of the appropriate bus company. Enquiries may be made at:
Buchanan Bus Station
(041) 332 9644 ext 233
daily 6:30am-10:15pm
Anderston Bus Station
(041) 248 7432
Mon-Sat 8am-5pm

rail
Central Station
(041) 332 9811 ext 4362
Mon-Sat 6:30am-11pm;
Sun 7:30am-11pm
Queen Street Station
(041) 332 9811 ext 3276
Mon-Fri 7am-10pm;
Sat 7am-8pm

air
Glasgow Airport
(041) 887 1111 (lost property desk ext *4558*)

city
Strathclyde Police Headquarters, Central Lost Property Office, 173 Pitt Street (enter by Holland Street) *(041) 204 2626*

MAIN POLICE STATIONS

Strathclyde Police Headquarters 173 Pitt Street G2 *(041) 204 2626*

divisional headquarters
(A) Stewart Street G4
    (041) 332 1113
(C) Maryhill Road G20
    (041) 946 1113
(D) Baird Street G4
    (041) 552 6333
(E) London Road G40
    (041) 554 1113
(F) Craigie Street G42
    (041) 423 1113
(G) Orkney Street G52
    (041) 445 1113

Partick Anderson Street G11 *(041) 339 1113*

CONSULATES

Australia
Hobart House
80 Hanover Street
Edinburgh EH2
(031) 226 6271

Belgium
91 Mitchell Street G1
(041) 248 5050

Brazil
6 Rose Street G3
(041) 332 6311

Costa Rica
18 Woodside Crescent G3
(041) 332 9755

Denmark
59 Waterloo Street G2
(041) 204 2209

France
11 Randolph Crescent
Edinburgh EH3
(031) 225 7954

West Germany
144 West George Street G2
(041) 331 2811

Greece
98 Baronald Drive G12
(041) 334 0360

Iceland
389 Argyle Street G2
(041) 221 6943

Italy
170 Hope Street G2
(041) 332 4297

Netherlands
102 Hope Street G2
(041) 221 0605

Norway
80 Oswald Street G1
(041) 204 1353

Pakistan
103 Bath Street G2
(041) 332 5544

Panama
Southwood Thomson Drive
Bearsden G61
(041) 942 1844

Peru
Flat 10 211 Nithsdale Road
G41 *(041) 423 7214*

Philippines
14 St Vincent Place G1
(041) 221 7552

Poland
27 Buckingham Terrace
G12 *(041) 334 4264*

South Africa
69 Nelson Mandela Place
G2 *(041) 221 3114*

Spain
389 Argyle Street G2
(041) 221 6943

Sweden
110 Bath Street G2
(041) 552 6552

Thailand
70 Wellington Street G2
(041) 248 6677

USA
3 Regent Terrace
Edinburgh EH7
(031) 556 8315

POST OFFICES

Head Office
George Square G2
(041) 248 2882
Mon-Thurs 8am-5:30pm
Fri 8:30am-5:30pm
Sat 9am-12:30pm

city branch offices

Charing Cross
533 Sauchiehall Street G3
(041) 221 5529

Dixon Street G1
(041) 248 6736

Gorbals
6/8 Cumberland Arcade G5
(041) 429 6351

Hope Street
216 Hope Street G2
(041) 332 4598

St Rollox
18 Glebe Street G4
(041) 552 4674

BANKS

Allied Irish Bank
1/3 Royal Exchange Square
G1 *(041) 226 4421*

Bank of England
25 St Vincent Place G1
(041) 221 7972

Bank of India
142a St Vincent Street G2
(041) 221 4153

Bank of Ireland
19 St Vincent Place G1
(041) 221 9353

Bank of Nova Scotia
52 West Nile Street G1
(041) 221 9171

Bank of Scotland
110 St Vincent Street G2
(041) 221 7071

Barclays Bank
90 St Vincent Street G2
(041) 221 9585

British Linen Bank
110 St Vincent Street G2
(041) 221 6692

Clydesdale Bank
30 St Vincent Place G1
(041) 248 7070

Co-operative Bank
47 St Vincent Street G2
(041) 248 3388

Hill Samuel
23 St Vincent Place G1
(041) 226 5331

Lloyds Bank
12 Bothwell Street G2
(041) 248 4661

National Bank of Pakistan
522 Sauchiehall Street G2
(041) 333 9599

National Westminster Bank
14 Blythswood Square G2
(041) 221 6981

Royal Bank of Scotland
98 Buchanan Street G1
(041) 248 2777

Standard Chartered Bank
14 West George Street G2
(041) 332 1514

Trustee Savings Bank
177 Ingram Street G1
(041) 552 6244

bank opening hours

Mon-Fri 9:30am-3:30pm,
with extended hours on
certain days

Smaller branches close
12:30pm-1:30pm
Saturdays

Barclays Bank
90 St Vincent Street
9:30am-12 noon

Lloyds Bank
in Lewis's Department
Store *(041) 204 1624*
9:30am-5pm

TSB
9-11 Renfield Street
9:30am- 4pm

bureaux de change
outside banking hours

Thomas Cook
15 Gordon Street G1
(041) 221 9431
Mon, Tues, Thurs, Fri 9am-
5:15pm
Wed 9:30am-5:15pm
Sat 9am-4:30pm

12 Moss Street Paisley
(041) 887 0424
Mon-Fri 9am-5:30pm
Sat 9am-4pm

A T Mays
90 Queen Street G1
(041) 221 0404/6048
Mon-Fri 9am-5:30pm
(closes 5pm Wed)
Sat 9am-5pm

American Express
115 Hope Street G2
(041) 226 3077
Mon-Fri 9am-5pm
Sat 9am-12 noon

British Rail
Central Station
(041) 226 5100 8am-8pm
Queen Street Station
(041) 332 9811 7am-11pm

PUBLIC LAVATORIES

City Centre
&281a West Campbell
Street
&5 Blythswood Street
&43 St Vincent Place
&77 St Enoch Square
Jocelyn Square — at
Saltmarket
71 Wilson Street
293 Clyde Street
&1 Cathedral Square

West End
Charing Cross —
1a Woodside Crescent
65 Cresswell Street

East End
1 Bridgeton Cross

South Side
1 Govan Cross
&Pollok Shopping Centre —
45 Cowglen Road
Shawlands Arcade —
50 Shawlands Square

HEALTH AND
EMERGENCY SERVICES

**Greater Glasgow Health
Board**
225 Bath Street G2
(041) 204 2755

Blood Transfusion Service
80 St Vincent Street G2
(041) 226 4111

**Charing Cross (Alcohol and
Drugs) Clinic**
8 Woodside Crescent G3
(041) 332 5463

Family Planning Centre
2 Claremont Terrace G1
(041) 332 9144

**St Andrews Ambulance
Association**
48 Milton Street G4
(041) 332 4031

**Scottish Ambulance
Headquarters**
Maitland Street G4
(041) 332 7080

hospitals
*has emergency department

Belvidere Hospital
London Road G31
(041) 554 1855

Dental Hospital and School
378 Sauchiehall Street G2
(041) 332 7020

Eastern District Hospital
Duke Street G31
(041) 556 5222

Eye Infirmary
3 Sandyford Place G3
(041) 204 0721

Gartnavel General Hospital
Great Western Road G12
(041) 334 8122

Gartnavel Royal Hospital
Great Western Road G12
(041) 334 6241

Homoeopathic Hospital
1000 Great Western Road
G12 *(041) 339 0382*

**Prince and Princess of Wales
Hospice, The**
71-73 Carlton Place G5
(041) 429 5599

Queen Mother, The
Yorkhill G3
(041) 339 8888

**Royal Beatson Memorial
Hospital**
132 Hill Street G3
(041) 332 0286

***Royal Hospital for Sick
Children**
(Yorkhill) G3
(041) 339 8888

*Royal Infirmary
84 Castle Street G4
(041) 552 3535

Royal Maternity Hospital
Rottenrow G4
(041) 552 3400

Royal Samaritan Hospital
for Women
Coplaw Street G42
(041) 423 3033

Ruchill Hospital
Bilsland Drive G20
(041) 946 7120

*Southern General Hospital
1345 Govan Road G51
(041) 445 2466

*Stobhill General Hospital
Balornock Road G21
(041) 558 0111

*Victoria Infirmary
Langside Road G42
(041) 649 4545

*Western Infirmary
Dumbarton Road G11
(041) 339 8822

health centres

Gorbals
Pine Place G5
(041) 429 6291

Govan
Langlands Road G51
(041) 440 1212

Maryhill
41 Shawpark Street G20
(041) 946 7151

Possilpark
Denmark Street G22
(041) 336 5311

Springburn
Springburn Road G21
(041) 558 0101

Townhead
16 Alexandra Parade G31
(041) 552 3477

Woodside
Barr Street G20
(041) 332 9977

Sunday and late-opening chemists

Bannerman
1851 Paisley Road West
Cardonald *(041) 882 1513*
(South side of Clyde
Tunnel) open 9am-9pm
every day of the year

R H Brown
259 Alderman Road G13
(041) 959 1914 9am-11pm
7 days a week; 693 Great
Western Road G12
(041) 339 0012 9am-9pm
7 days a week; 77 Lochend
Road G34 (Easterhouse)
(041) 773 2003 9am-9pm
Mon-Sat, 10am-9pm
Sunday; 128 Saracen Street
G22 *(041) 336 8561* 9am-
9pm 7 days a week

C & M Mackie
1067 Pollokshaws Road
G41 (Shawlands Cross)
(041) 649 8915 open 9am-
8pm Mon-Fri, 9am-6pm Sat,
11am-6pm Sun, 12-3pm all
public holidays

T S McNee
2 Springburn Way G21
(041) 558 5209 open 9am-
9pm Mon-Fri, 9:30am-
5:30pm Saturday, 12-5pm
Sunday, 10am-5pm all
public holidays

Most chemists operate a
rota for weekend
dispensing; information
from: Primary Care
Department, Greater
Glasgow Health Board 225
Bath Street G2
(041) 204 2755
For emergency
prescriptions overnight or
at weekends contact the
police.

ANIMAL WELFARE

Glasgow and West of
Scotland Society for the
Prevention of Cruelty to
Animals
15 Royal Terrace G3
(041) 332 0716 (or phone
police *(041) 204 2626*)

Royal Society for the
Protection of Birds
Lochwinnoch Nature
Centre, Largs Road,
Lochwinnoch
Lochwinnoch 842663

People's Dispensary for Sick
Animals
1 Shamrock Street G4
(041) 332 6944

Dog and Cat Home
Corkerhill *(041) 882 1688*

kennels

Glendale Kennels
Drumkinnay Farm Balloch
Alexandria 52318

Oscar's Country Farm for
Dogs and Cats
Barriston Farm Torrance
Balmore 20535

ON THIS SITE
STOOD THE SURGICAL WARDS
IN WHICH FROM 1861 TO 1869
JOSEPH LISTER
SURGEON TO THE ROYAL INFIRMARY
AND REGIUS PROFESSOR OF SURGERY
IN THE UNIVERSITY OF GLASGOW
INITIATED THE METHOD OF
ANTISEPTIC TREATMENT

PLACES OF WORSHIP AND RELIGIOUS BODIES

Adelaide Place Baptist Church
209 Bath Street G2
(041) 248 4970

Anderston Kelvingrove Parish Church
Argyle Street G3
(041) 221 9408

Catholic Church Archdiocesan Office
18 Park Circus G3
(041) 332 9473

Central Mosque
Islamic Centre
Adelphi Street G5
(041) 429 7171/3132

Church of Scotland Prebytery of Glasgow
260 Bath Street G2
(041) 332 6606

Episcopal Church in Scotland
5 St Vincent Place G1
(041) 221 5720

First Church of Christ, Scientist
1 La Belle Place G3
(041) 332 8046

Garnethill Synagogue
29 Garnet Street G3
(041) 332 4151

Glasgow Buddhist Centre
329 Sauchiehall Street G2
(041) 333 0524

Glasgow Cathedral
Castle Street G4
(041) 552 0220

Gorbals Church
5 Cumberland Street G5
(041) 429 5494

Queen's Park Synagogue
Communal Hall
Falloch Road G42
(041) 632 2139

Religious Society of Friends (Quakers)
16 Newton Terrace G3
(041) 221 7770

Renfield St Stephens Church Centre
260 Bath Street G2
(041) 332 4293

St Aloysius
(Roman Catholic) Hill Street
Garnethill G3
(041) 332 3039

St Andrews Cathedral
(Roman Catholic) 190
Clyde Street G1
(041) 221 3096

St Columba Church
337 West George Lane G2
(041) 221 3305

St Georges Tron Parish Church
165 Buchanan Street G2
(041) 221 2141

St Mary's Cathedral
(Episcopal) Great Western
Road *(041) 339 4956*
(rectory)

St Vincent Street Free Church of Scotland
265 St Vincent Street G2
(041) 221 1937

Salvation Army
67 Carlton Place G5
(041) 429 0532

Theosophical Society of Scotland
17 Queens Crescent G4
(041) 332 4924

UK Islamic Mission
Mosque and Islamic Centre,
19 Carrington Street G4
(041) 332 2811 or *331 1119*

United Free Church of Scotland
11 Newton Place G3
(041) 332 3435

SPORTS

For information on sports marked * apply to **Sports Council for Glasgow** 20 Trongate G1 *(041) 227 5068*; for other sports see below.

  aeromodelling
*aikido
*American football
  angling
*archery
*athletics
*badminton
*basketball
*baton-twirling
  billiards, snooker
  BMX (bicycle motocross)
  board sailing
  boating
*bowling (see also below)
  indoor
  outdoor
*boxing
  canoeing
*car clubs
  clay pigeons
*cricket
*croquet
*cross-country
*curling
*cycling
*dancing — country
  — natural
*diving
*fencing
  fishing — see angling
  flying
*football
  gliding
  golf
  public courses
  clubs
*gymnastics
*handball
*hang gliding
*hockey
  roller hockey — see below
*judo
*karate
*kayak
*keep fit
  kendo
*lacrosse
*motocross
*mountaineering
*netball
*orienteering

  sports parachuting
  putting greens
  racing
  dogs
  horses
  riding
  roller hockey
*rowing
*rugby
*running
*sailing
*shooting
  skating
*skiing
  snooker — see billiards
*squash
*sub-aqua
*swimming pools (see also below)
  public
  private
*table tennis
*tae kwon do
*tennis
*trampolining
*volleyball
  walking/rambling
  water-skiing
*weightlifting
*wrestling

Kelvin Hall Sports and Recreation Complex
Kelvingrove G3
In 1985 the Kelvin Hall was superseded by the Scottish Exhibition and Conference Centre (see p. 86) as Glasgow's main venue for major exhibitions and other events. In future the building will serve two purposes: it will house the new Museum of Transport (see p. 39) and it will provide Glasgow with a new sports centre of international standing (scheduled to open late autumn 1987).

The Centre will have an Athletics Hall with a 200-metre running track of international standard and capacity for 5 000 spectators. There will be two other sports halls, each with space for 1 500 spectators, as well as numerous supporting amenities and services.

The Kelvin Hall's central site, opposite the Art Gallery and Museum in Kelvingrove Park, makes it ideal for major sporting events as well as for use by the large local community.

sports centres

Alexandra
Alexandra Parade
Dennistoun
(041) 556 1695

Bellahouston
Bellahouston Drive
Bellahouston
(041) 427 5454

Burnhill
Toryglen Road Rutherglen
(041) 643 0327

Helenvale
Helenvale Street Parkhead
G31 *(041) 554 4109*

James Murray
Caledonia Road Baillieston
(041) 773 0881

Maryhill Sports Centre
60 Burnhouse Street
Maryhill G20
(041) 946 2354

Pollokshaws
Ashtree Road Pollokshaws
(041) 632 2200

Shettleston
Elvan Street Shettleston
G32 *(041) 778 1346*

Crownpoint Road Sports Park
Crownpoint Road Bridgeton
(041) 554 8274

aeromodelling

Scottish Aeromodellers
Association *(041) 883 2655*

angling

game: Scottish National
Anglers Association
(041) 221 7206

coarse: Scottish Federation
of Coarse Anglers
(0505) 862 460

sea: Scottish Federation of
Sea Anglers 18 Ainslie
Place Edinburgh EH3
(031) 225 7611

billiards and snooker

Scottish Billiards Association
(041) 883 2325

BMX
(bicycle motocross)

Scottish BMX
(041) 558 2613

board sailing

Scottish Board Sailing
Association *(0546) 2024*

boating

Glasgow District Council,
Parks and Recreation
Department *(041) 227 5066*

bowling

outdoor
most public parks have
bowling greens (phone
Parks and Recreation as
above)

indoor
Scottish Indoor Bowling
Association *(0294) 68372*

canoeing

Scottish Canoe Association
(031) 226 4401

clay pigeon shooting

West of Scotland Shooting
School, Bankell Farm,
Strathblane Road, Milngavie
G62 *(041) 956 1733* (game
shooting by arrangement);
see also **shooting**

flying

Glasgow Flying Club
Glasgow Airport
(041) 887 1111

gliding

Strathclyde Gliding Club
(041) 481 3476

golf

public courses
(Glasgow District Council,
Parks and Recreation
Department *(041) 227 5066*)

18-hole
    Lethamhill Golf Course,
    Cumbernauld Road,
    Millerston
Linn Park, Simshill Road
Littlehill Golf Course,
    Auchinairn Road,
    Bishopbriggs

9-hole
    Alexandra Park,
    Provan Road
King's Park,
    Carmunnock Road
Knightswood Park,
    Bassett Avenue
Ruchill Park,
    Bilsland Drive

clubs
Scottish Golf Union, 54
Shandwick Place,
Edinburgh EH2
(031) 226 6711

kendo

British Kendo Association
(01) 644 1369

sports parachuting

(031) 557 0571

putting greens

most public parks have
putting greens (Glasgow
District Council, Parks and
Recreation Department
(041) 227 5066)

racing

horse racing

Ayr Race Course, Whitletts
Road, Ayr *(0292) 262340*

Hamilton Race Course,
Hamilton *(7 from Glasgow)*
283806

greyhound racing

Shawfield Stadium,
Rutherglen *(041) 647 4121*

riding

British Horse Society
(050) 587 2682

Busby Equitation Centre
Wester Farm, Busby
(041) 644 1347

Hazelden School of
Equitation, Hazelden Road,
Mearnskirk, Newton
Mearns G77 *(041) 639 3011*

Kilmardinny Riding Stables,
Kilmardinny Farm,
Milngavie Road, Bearsden
G61 *(041) 943 1310*

roller hockey

National Roller Hockey
Association *(0472) 361240*

skating

The Summit Centre
Minerva Way, Finnieston
(041) 204 2215

Scottish Ice Figure Skating
Association, Murrayfield Ice
Rink, Edinburgh EH12
(031) 337 3976

snooker

see **billiards**

swimming pools

Glasgow District Council,
Parks and Recreation
Department *(041) 227 5066*

Castlemilk
137 Castlemilk Drive G45
(041) 634 8254

Drumchapel
199 Drumry Road East G15
(041) 944 5812

Easterhouse
Bogbain Road G34
(041) 771 7978

Govan Fun Pool
Harhill Street G51
(041) 445 1899

Govanhill
99 Calder Street G42
(041) 423 0233

Maryhill
60 Burnhouse Street G20
(041) 946 2354

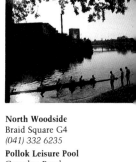

North Woodside
Braid Square G4
(041) 332 6235

Pollok Leisure Pool
Cowglen Road
(041) 881 3313

Pollokshaws
Ashtree Road G43
(041) 632 2200

Rutherglen
44 Greenhill Road
Rutherglen *(041) 647 4530*

Shettleston
Elvan Street G32
(041) 778 1346

Temple
Knightscliffe Avenue G13
(041) 954 6537

Whitehill
Onslow Drive G31
(041) 551 9969

Whiteinch
Medwyn Street G14
(041) 959 2465

Whitevale
81 Whitevale Street G31
(041) 554 0695

walking/rambling

Glasgow District Council,
Parks and Recreation
Department *(041) 227 5066*

Countryside Ranger, Pollok
Park *(041) 632 9299*

Ramblers Association
(041) 956 2642

water skiing

Chief Instructor — Water
Sports, Strathclyde Park
(60 from Glasgow) 66155
ext *59*

**Glasgow Marathon
crossing the Clyde**

ENTERTAINMENTS

theatres and concert halls see p. 43

cinemas

Cannon Film Centre
326 Sauchiehall Street G2
(041) 332 1592 or
(programme only) *9513*

&**Glasgow Film Theatre**
12 Rose Street G3
(041) 332 6535

Grosvenor Cinema
Ashton Lane off Byres
Road G12 *(041) 339 4298*

Odeon Film Centre
56 Renfield Street G2
(041) 332 8701

&**Salon Cinema**
Vinicombe Street off
Byres Road G12
(041) 339 4256

discotheques, dance halls, nightclubs

Glasgow has many places
where one may find
evening entertainment and
the following list is a short
selection of these. For
information on others, see
local press, in particular the
Evening Times and *The
List* (see p. 87).

Bennetts
90 Glassford Street G1
(041) 552 5761

Cardinal Folly
193 Pitt Street G2
(041) 332 1111

Cleopatras
508 Great Western Road
G3 *(041) 334 0560*

Cotton Club
5 Scott Street
(041) 332 0712

Daddy Warbucks
46 West George Street
(041) 332 0122

Henry Afrikas
15 York Street G2
(041) 221 6111

Kelvin Centre
1073 Argyle Street G3
(041) 221 4001

Joe Paparazzi
520 Sauchiehall Street G2
(041) 331 2111

Lucifers
22 Jamaica Street G1
(041) 248 4600

Mardi Gras
81-85 Dunlop Street G1
(041) 248 7810

Mayfair
490 Sauchiehall Street G2
(041) 332 3872

Panama Jax
Custom House Quay G1
(041) 221 0865

Pzazz
23 Royal Exchange Square
G1 *(041) 221 5323*

Raffles
15 Benalder Street
(041) 334 5321

Rooftops
92 Sauchiehall Street G2
(041) 332 5883

Savoy
Savoy Centre Sauchiehall
Street G2 *(041) 332 0751*

ACCOMMODATION

There is a wide range of
accommodation available in
Glasgow, at all price levels.
A small guidebook could
not begin to give adequate
details on all of these but
the **Greater Glasgow Tourist
Board** provides an excellent
information service. Their
opening hours are generous,
especially in the tourist
season (see p. 69).

Information is available
not only on international
hotels — and several, such
as the Holiday Inn and
Hospitality Inn, are
represented in Glasgow —
but also on smaller hotels
throughout the city, on
guest houses and private
houses, and on self-catering
accommodation. Both self-
catering and rooms with
service are available in
vacation time in some of
the halls of residence of the
universities and colleges.

GGTB will send a list of
any category on request.

Scottish Youth Hostels
Association, Glasgow
District Office, 12 Renfield
Street G2 *(041) 226 3976*

Glasgow Youth Hostel 10
Woodlands Terrace G3
(041) 332 3004

An independent hostel
operates during the
university vacation (late
July to mid September):
Glasgow Central Tourist
Hostel, Balmanno Building,
81 Rottenrow East
(041) 552 2401

PLACES TO EAT AND DRINK

This book cannot be an exhaustive guide to Glasgow's growing number of good restaurants and pubs and the following list simply gives a few suggestions, divided into national sections.

* indicates the more expensive restaurants. Further information is available from the **Greater Glasgow Tourist Board** (*(041) 227 4880* who will provide a more comprehensive list.

general

Babbity Bowster's
16-18 Blackfriars Street G1
(041) 552 5055

*Buttery
652 Argyle Street G3
(041) 221 8188

*Colonial
25 High Street G1
(041) 552 1923

*Diva
7 Park Terrace
(041) 332 3520

Cafe Gandolfi
Albion Street
(041) 552 6813

Granary (Health Food) Restaurant
82 Howard Street G1
(041) 226 3770

Grosvenor Café
33 Ashton Lane G12
(041) 339 1848

*Poachers
Ruthven Lane G12
(041) 339 0932

*Rogano
11 Exchange Place G1
(041) 248 4055

Third Eye Centre
see p. 41

*Ubiquitous Chip
12 Ashton Lane G12
(041) 334 5007

Indian

Asha Indian Vegetarian Restaurant
415 Sauchiehall Street G2
(041) 332 5018

Koh-i-Noor
235 North Street G3
(041) 204 1444

Shish Mahal
41-47 Gibson Street G12
(041) 334 7899

Chinese

Amber Royale
336 Argyle Street

Loon Fung
417 Sauchiehall Street G3
(041) 332 1240

Italian

Ristorante Caprese
217 Buchanan Street G1
(041) 332 3070

La Costiera
51 West Regent Street G2
(041) 331 1980

La Lanterna
35 Hope Street G2
(041) 221 9160

Spaghetti Factory
30 Gibson Street G12
(041) 334 2665

French

Café Noir
151 Queen Street G1
(041) 248 3525

Fouquets Wine Bar
7 Renfield Street G2
(041) 226 4958

Lautrecs Wine Bar Brasserie
14 Woodlands Terrace G3
(041) 332 7013

American

Ad Lib
111 Hope Street G2
(041) 221 8991

CARAVAN AND CAMPSITES

Barnbrock Camping Site
Barnbrock Farm,
Kilbarchan, Renfrewshire
*Bridge of Weir (4 from
Glasgow) 690915*

Hogganfield Caravan Site
1563 Cumbernauld Road,
Millerston G33
*(041) 770 5602 or (evenings)
(041) 776 3020*

Kilmardinny Riding Centre
(tents and caravans)
Milngavie Road, Bearsden
G42 *(041) 942 4404*

Lagganbeg Caravan Park
Gartocharn *(038 983) 281*

Tullichewan Caravan Park
(also tents) Old Luss Road,
Balloch, Dunbartonshire
G83 *(0389) 59475*

CARAVAN HIRE

Cabervans
Caberfeidh, Cloch Road,
Gourock PA19
(0475) 38775

Melville's Self Drive
4 Hill Drive, Eaglesham
G76 *(560 from Glasgow)
2589*

CONFERENCE AND EXHIBITION CENTRES

Being at the hub of a
densely populated area,
Glasgow is an ideal location
for any exhibition,
conference or product
launch and it now has a
large number of modern
well-equipped venues. The
**Greater Glasgow Convention
Bureau** 35/39 St Vincent
Place G1 *(041) 227 4885*
provides information on
any of these for
conventions of any size and
offers services in the
following aspects:

conference venue
selection

facility visits
site inspection
accommodation booking
  service
local and in-bound
  transportation
pre- and post-convention
  tours
civic hospitality
social programme
tourist information
multi-lingual tourist
  guides

**Scottish Exhibition and
Conference Centre** G3
(041) 248 3000
Opened in 1985, the SECC
is one of the world's best
and most up-to-date
conference centres. It
occupies a 64-acre site on
the north bank of the Clyde
at Stobcross Quay, not only
close to the city centre but
highly accessible to all
forms of transport, by road,
rail, or air.

CULTURAL ORGANISATIONS

Book Trust Scotland
(formerly the National Book
League) 15a Lynedoch
Street G3 *(041) 332 0391*
for book information and
promotion, specialising in
Scottish and children's
books.

British Council
6 Belmont Crescent G12
(041) 339 8651

French Institute
7 Bowmont Gardens G12
(041) 357 3632
French cultural organisation
(a branch of the French
Ministry of Foreign Affairs);
runs classes, exhibitions,
social events etc.

Goethe-Institut Glasgow
(formerly the Scottish-
German Centre) Lower
Medway Building, 74
Victoria Crescent Road G12
(041) 334 6116

German cultural organisation, roughly equivalent of the British Council; runs classes, exhibitions, social events etc.

Mayfest Ltd
46 Royal Exchange Square G1 *(041) 221 4911*
Runs an annual international festival of the arts.

Scottish Ballet
261 West Princes Street G4 *(041) 331 2931*

Scottish Early Music Consort
c/o Mrs Jan Crook,
73 Glasserton Road G43 *(041) 637 5019*

Scottish Music Information Centre
7 Lilybank Gardens G12 *(041) 334 6393*

Scottish National Orchestra
3 La Belle Place Glasgow G3 *(041) 332 7244*

Scottish Opera
39 Elmbank Crescent G2 *(041) 332 3321*

NEWSPAPERS AND PERIODICALS

Gairm
29 Waterloo Street G2 *(041) 221 1971*
Gaelic quarterly magazine.

Glasgow Herald
195 Albion Street G1 *(041) 552 6255*
As well as wide news coverage, it is a good source of general information and advertisement. Main day for property advertising is Tuesday and for business properties and extensive business news, Wednesday. Friday's paper carries the largest number of job advertisements. Theatre notices daily. Auction sales Monday.

Glasgow Evening Times
as above (sister paper). Main source of advertisements. Cinema notices. Property Tuesday. Car sales Friday.

The Glaswegian
128 Elderslie Street G3 *(041) 248 3364*
General-interest monthly magazine.

Gloss
50 Wellington Street G2 *(041) 248 7799*
Free fashion and general-interest magazine for Glasgow and Edinburgh.

Jewish Echo
463 Eglinton Street G5 *(041) 429 2034*
Weekly paper for the Jewish community.

The List
14 High Street Edinburgh EH1 *(031) 558 1191*
Fortnightly Glasgow and Edinburgh events guide.

Scotsman Publications
78 Queen Street G1 *(041) 221 6485*

Scottish Catholic Observer
19 Waterloo Street G2 *(041) 221 4956*

Scottish Daily Express
Park House, Park Circus Place G3 *(041) 332 9600*

Scottish Daily Record and Sunday Mail
Anderston Quay *(041) 248 7000*

Sunday Post
144 Port Dundas Road G4 *(041) 332 9933*

Urdu Adab
26 Bank Street G12 *(041) 229 5513*
English and Urdu Asian quarterly for Glasgow.

What's On
20 Renfrew Street G2 *(041) 333 0471*
Monthly list of events and facilities in Scotland.

RADIO AND TELEVISION

BBC
Broadcasting House, Queen Margaret Drive G12 *(041) 339 8844*

Radio Clyde PLC
Clydebank Business Park South Avenue Clydebank *(041) 941 1111*

Scottish Television PLC
Cowcaddens G2 *(041) 332 9999*

GENERAL INFORMATION

area of city 76 square miles

population 740 000

early closing days Tuesday or Saturday, though many shops in the centre operate a six- or even seven-day week.

telephone services NB the Glasgow dialling code is *041*; do not use when making local calls.
time: dial *123* on any telephone
weather forecast *(041) 246 8091*
Marineline:
  Clyde forecast
  (041) 552 4466
  Caledonia forecast
  (041) 552 4477
Mountainline forecast *(041) 248 5757*
Automobile Association *(041) 812 0101*
Coastguard (Greenock) *(0475) 29988* (to contact ships at sea).

DISTANCES FROM GLASGOW

	miles
Aberdeen	143
Birmingham	292
Bristol	371
Cambridge	351
Carlisle	95
Dover	488
Edinburgh	45
Fort William	105
Hull	245
Inverness	172
John o' Groats	299
Kendal	147
Land's End	573
Liverpool	221
London	402
Manchester	214
Newcastle	150
Norwich	379
Oxford	357
Penzance	562
Perth	60
Southampton	429
Stranraer	93
York	208

SOURCES OF INFORMATION AND OTHER USEFUL ADDRESSES

Greater Glasgow Tourist Board, 35-39 St Vincent Place G1 *(041) 227 4880*

Glasgow District Council, Public Relations Department, City Chambers, George Square G2 *(041) 227 4157/8/9*

Strathclyde Regional Headquarters, 20 India Street G2 *(041) 204 2900*

Citizen's Advice Bureau, 212 Bath Street G2 *(041) 331 2345*

Mitchell Library, North Street G3 *(041) 221 7030* see also p. 00

National Trust for Scotland, Hutchesons' Hospital Hall, 158 Ingram Street G1 *(041) 552 8391*

BOOK LIST

general

Barr, W W *Discovering Glasgow* Glasgow 1980

Barr, W W *Ghosts of Glasgow* Glasgow 1982

Barr, W W *Glasgwegiana* Glasgow 1973

Baxter, Colin *Experience Scotland: Glasgow* 1986

Cant, R G and Lindsay, I G *Old Glasgow* Edinburgh 1947

Daiches, David *Glasgow* London 1977

Defoe, Daniel *A Tour thro' the Whole Island of Great Britain* ed G D H Cole, London 1927

Checkland, S G *The Upas Tree Glasgow 1875-1975* Glasgow 1976

Eyre-Todd, George and Renwick, Robert *History of Glasgow* (3 vols) Glasgow 1921-34

House, Jack *Glasgow Old and New* Glasgow 1974

House, Jack *The Heart of Glasgow* Glasgow 1965

House, Jack *Music Hall Memories* Glasgow 1986

Jocelin of Furness *Life of St Kentigern* (ed Forbes in *Historians of Scotland* 1874)

Lindsay, Maurice *Portrait of Glasgow* London 1972

M'Dowall, John K *The People's History of Glasgow* Glasgow 1899

Mackie, J D *The University of Glasgow, 1451-1951* 1954

McUre, John *History of Glasgow* Glasgow 1736

Morris, William *A Walk through Glasgow Cathedral* Glasgow 1986

Moss, M and Hume J *Glasgow as It Was* 1975

Munro, Michael *The Patter: A guide to current Glasgow usage* Glasgow 1985

Oakley, C A *The Second City* Glasgow 1946

Reid, J M *Glasgow* London 1956

Senex (Robert Reid) *Glasgow Past and Present* 1884

museums, art, architecture

Bilcliffe, Roger *Architectural Sketches and Flower Drawings of Charles Rennie Mackintosh* London 1977

Bilcliffe, Roger *Charles Rennie Mackintosh: The Complete Furniture, Furniture Drawings and Interior Design* London 1979

The Burrell Collection London and Glasgow 1983

Gomme, Andor and Walker, David *The Architecture of Glasgow* London 1968

Howarth, Thomas *Charles Rennie Mackintosh and the Modern Movement* London 1953

Kenna, Rudolph *Glasgow Art Deco* Glasgow 1985

King, Elspeth *The People's Palace and Glasgow Green* Glasgow 1985

Larner, Gerald and Celia *The Glasgow Style* Edinburgh 1979

Macleod, Robert *Charles Rennie Mackintosh* London 1968

Marks, Richard *Burrell: A Portrait of a Collector* Glasgow 1983

Marks, Richard *Souvenir Guide to the Burrell Collection* Glasgow 1985

McLaren Young, Andrew and Doak, A M *Glasgow at a Glance: an architectural handbook* (revised edition) Glasgow 1965

INDEX